THE
ART NOUVEAU
DACHA

Designs by

VLADIMIR STORY

Edited by

Peter Nasmyth

In an association with

The International Network for
Traditional Building, Architecture and Urbanism

Published by
Mta Publications
London

Published by

Mta Publications
27 Old Gloucester Street
LONDON WC1N 3AX

www.mtapublications.co.uk
Email: inquiry@mtapublications.co.uk

Originally published by
The Strakun Publishing House
St Petersburg, 1917

Cover design Victoria Kirkham

ISBN 978-0-9559145-2-2

ACKNOWLEDGEMENTS
Special thanks to Matthew Hardy of INTBAU, Kate Hughes, Emily Maitland,
Maia Mania, Anna Matveeva, Manana Moniava, Donald Rayfield, Jane
Samuels, Peter Simon, Amy Spurling, Katya Turgeneva, Yelena Zagrevskaya

FOREWORD

HRH, The Prince of Wales

CLARENCE HOUSE

Russia has a remarkable and ancient tradition of wooden buildings that dates back to the tenth century, with the remains of Medieval fortresses demonstrating the sophistication of the Nordic wooden construction methods employed across Russia and Scandinavia at the time. In the eighteenth century, Peter the Great's policy of broader cultural engagement between Russia and the rest of Europe stimulated cultural influence both to and from Russia, finding its way into the rich urban and architectural language of the time. Rather than destroying local traditions, which has happened with the prevalence of the International Style since the 1950's, the various traditions were fused and reinterpreted giving rise to the new living traditions in building we enjoy so much today.

As George Heard Hamilton observed:

"In the 19th century the Russians did not invent the forms of narrative poem, novel, symphony or opera; but Pushkin and Tolstoy, Tchaikovsky and Mussorgsky used the technical means common to European art to create works inimitably Russian which we number among the masterpieces of world literature and music."

Nowhere is this wonderful fusion of ideas more neatly demonstrated than in the Russian *Dacha,* a tradition of building small timber houses as rural retreats on the outskirts of the city for the summer months. As these areas of retreat became more populated, often laid out along railway lines, and the structures themselves more aspirational, they became populated year round.

These intriguing building types, featured in the republication of Vladimir Story's original catalogue, show us in a microcosm how European regional influences have been fused with local construction methods to give an Art Nouveau style layered with something unmistakably Russian.

It is heartening that Anton Glikin, who graduated from my Institute of Architecture, has brought this work back to life and, hopefully, people will take inspiration in reviving these important traditions of settlement to meet the challenges that living sustainably on the planet now presents.

INTRODUCTION

– 4 –

The Russian Dacha

THE story of the Russian dacha is a tale of design evolution mixed with the human desire to engage with nature. While both instincts may be universal, they show particular prominence in Russia, a country that today possesses the highest ownership of second homes in the world. This fact is due almost entirely to its remarkable history of dacha culture. Even during the Soviet period when the concept of private property had been all but abolished by the state, dacha ownership and building continued unabated, being so deeply ingrained.

Originally set up during the reign of Peter the Great as a rural release for the aristocracy ('dacha' comes from the word meaning 'gift,' as many were given by the Tsar to his loyal workers), the dacha fashion quickly caught on. By the end of the 19th Century dacha ownership became a common aspiration of the developing middle classes. Many of Russia's larger cities became steadily ringed with enclaves of these small, individually designed and charming homesteads. At times their gardens would carry almost equal importance to the houses, becoming miniature growing empires for each family. Furthermore, the dacha came to serve as the centre-stage for many of Russian literature's greatest dramas. Writers like Dostoyevsky, Chekhov, Pasternak, Gorky not only set their stories in dachas, they also wrote them in dachas.

The arrival of Art Nouveau in Russia at the turn of the 20th Century added powerful new elements to the local architecture. These had found their inspiration within the naturalistic design features developed by men like William Morris, as they combined with the new technologies and materials. Buildings like Moscow's grand Yaroslavsky railway station (1902-4) heralded the arrival of the bold new 'Modern' style (as Art Nouveau was called in Russia after the French term *Moderne*). Elements such as its innovative curved roof appealed instinctively to the public eye. Modern designs began appearing in architectural 'pattern books' like this one, offering the style to the buying public in catalogue form. In so doing, these books helped popularise the movement, particularly around the larger population centres. While in cities Art Nouveau buildings would often incorporate elaborate sculptural motifs, their more modest country cousins – the dachas – presented the originality of the movement in a simpler, but no less appealing architecture.

In post-Revolutionary Russia the Constructivists and Classicists took over and the 'bourgeois' Art Nouveau designs disappeared quickly. However, its short heyday during the first two decades of the 20th century produced many striking dwellings, although many have since disappeared. This book by Vladimir Gotlibovich Story is a priceless record of a particularly rich period of the architectural imagination, a time in which design celebrated the curves and asymmetry of nature within the very structure of buildings. Today we find elements of this style of wooden house-building returning to fashion as a means of combining the more ecological aspects of design with the aesthetic.

Dacha Life

At the turn of the 20th Century the notion of 'the dacha' already lay deep within the common imagination. Architects set out to generate a rural atmosphere of relaxation and relative classlessness in which people from all walks of life lived together, while served by the new modern technologies such as the railway. Memoirs written from Leningrad in 1976 by two elderly gentlemen, D.I. Zasosov and V.I. Pizin, describe Siverskaya, a village near St. Petersburg, as *'the kind of dacha settlement that could satisfy modest clerks, rich tenants, artists, poets, aristocrats – people with various budgets'.* In such places the grander dachas were owned by aristocrats, like the summer residence of Emperor Nicholas II's minister to the Imperial Court, Baron Vladimir Borisovich Friederichs (descendant of a Swedish officer captured by Peter the Great). These still carried the air of the classic Russian *pomeschik* (Lord of the Manor) estate, at a time when all around them seething ideas of revolution began to grip the popular mind.

As a direct result this book, published in 1917, must be one of the last of its kind. The Revolution later that same year swept away all that had proceeded it in a hungry surge towards the 'new', which at that point nobody quite understood.

At the turn of the 20th Century the majority of dacha settlements in Russia resembled small suburban English villages, save that the houses were often owned by local farmers, prosperous landlords and developers. Most were rented seasonally, beginning in the late spring or early summer. But with dacha villages often laid out along railways, people increasingly visited them during the winter. This explains why many designs in these pages offer the choice of adding 'warm' areas to the house. State employees in the early 20th Century rarely received more than two weeks of holiday a year and those working in private business, such as banks, often none at all. This created the phenomenon of the *dachniy muzh* ('dacha husband') a type of family man who, during summer, commuted every day between his family in the dacha and work.

By the early 1900s developers intensified their purchase of lands around St. Petersburg and Moscow, repackaging then reselling them into smaller, compartmentalized plots. Dachas would quickly spring up, built following designs similar to those found in this book. The pre-Revolutionary dacha villages often wore the heavy garments of capitalism, with houses numbered in the order of purchase rather than location, and streets named after the developers: factors no doubt contributing to the 'dictatorship of the proletariat' that followed.

Those wishing to rent a summer dacha would usually make a house inspection in April, arriving on horse-harnessed sleighs. After the dacha had been viewed the tenant would accompany the owner to his house, where contract signing tended to be sealed by the customary shot of vodka. In May, at the end of the long Russian winter, city dwellers flocked to the countryside and the dacha season began in earnest. As Zasosov and Pizin described it:

> *[people arrived]... with backpacks, boxes, baskets, cats, dogs, volleyball bags, and... cages with birds. At the local railway station a luggage receipt would be given to the landlord meeting the new tenants. As they ascended a hill, an unknown man might suddenly clutch at the carriage saying: 'I am a baker, give me your address and I'll be delivering your fresh bread.'*

Around St Petersburg this great annual outflux to the countryside would extend to all levels of society. Even the beggars liked to reinvent themselves 'country style.' According to Zasosov and Pizin, such men suddenly became peasants whose *'houses had been destroyed by fire'*, and then would give *'long and graphic descriptions of the event'*.

Additionally, dachas became places of learning for children who failed their spring exams. Tutoring was usually offered by the older students and local fence posts would sprout advertisements for private tuition like an odd kind of spring flower. As technology continued to develop it generated ever-new fads among the tutors and other 'dachniks' (dacha residents), like the bicycle which became a popular, if expensive, form of transportation between homes and villages. In those days a bicycle could cost between 100–150 roubles while a three-room dacha would rent for 50–80 roubles per summer (80 roubles would then have been approximately $850 US today).

This sudden eruption of dacha life in the spring and summer extended into the dramatic arts. Barns were hired from farmers and converted into temporary summer theatres or dance floors. Grand pianos could be rented at 15 roubles per summer. Money from the tickets often went to local organizations such as the volunteer fire brigade, the only defence against the great fear of all dacha dwellers – house fires. Indeed, men like Duke Lvov would become President of the All Russian Firemen Volunteers Society.

The pastoral atmosphere of the dacha village could also inspire the aristocracy. In Ligovo a professional orchestra sponsored by Count Sheremetiev would play concerts in the middle of a lake, floating on a specially designed raft. The general public would suddenly encounter music while walking through the forests, taking picnics, or rowing across the water.

Large wooden pavilions often appeared within the dacha communities, such as at Martishkino near St Petersburg. Erected by the *'dachniks'* themselves, particularly those of German descent, they operated as gymnasiums, in keeping with the new fashion of gymnastic societies. These also contributed to the musical ambience of the countryside, as field trips *'were often accompanied by a beating drum to maintain good spirits'* (Zasosov, Pizin).

The aristocracy took the dacha culture to grander levels, especially round the Peterhof area of St Petersburg (known as the 'Russian Versailles'), which housed the higher-class residential dachas, usually for courtiers. *'The place felt like an imperial residence, in which guards dressed in Caucasian uniform paraded everywhere'* (Zasosov, Pizin). But even the Imperial Parks welcomed the public, where outdoor orchestras would often play for the general entertainment.

Vladimir Story

Unlike his more celebrated contemporary architects such as Fedor Shekhtel, Fedor Lidval, Ivan Fomin, Andrey Belogrud and Vladimir Schuko, Vladimir Story remains something of a mystery. Although he published his pattern books through the prominent M. G. Strakun Publishing House at Nevsky Prospect 32, no biographical references to him are found in the Academy of Fine Arts Archive, the Academy of Fine Arts Library, the St. Petersburg Public Library, New York Public Library, The British Library, or the State Historical Archive of St. Petersburg.

For the moment the best evidence of Vladimir Story's life is his pattern books (five were printed between 1907 and 1917) and buildings. How many still survive today is impossible to say, but this book does carry the engraving of what appears to be a completed dacha at Alexandrovskoye (see cover reproduction). Due to its late publication it is unlikely any of these designs made it beyond the drawing board. Story operated at a very difficult time for architects and professionals in general. As he designed his dachas in St Petersburg, the Russian Revolution whipped itself into a frenzy all around his office. Paper shortages bedevilled the publishing industry, as can be seen in the editorial remarks included in this edition's first pages, 'From the Editor'. It should be counted as a miracle that this book ever saw the far end of a printing press. Certainly it gives every impression of being a rushed production. The original Russian edition contains a number of mistakes and omissions. Some, but not all, have been corrected here.

But life and house-building had to continue. Like his more celebrated but perhaps less inventive contemporary Grigori Sudeykin, Story was happy to take on multiple commissions at relatively low prices, starting at 35 roubles – hence the book's subtitle 'Cheap Buildings.' He expressly describes himself as 'a building technician', and his architectural practice combined itself with a construction company. As a result Story was able to provide service-packages that included site supervision, mortgage consultancy, design, and the physical construction of dachas, tenements and factories.

The Art Nouveau Dacha

By the time this book was published in 1917, it is likely that many of its designs were already considered retrograde by Story's St. Petersburg architectural contemporaries. In 1910 Peter Behrens completed his German Embassy in triumphant neoclassical style. Around the same time Ivan Fomin contemptuously declared Art Nouveau a 'mercantile style', as he designed Neoclassical villas in and around the St. Petersburg region.

But Story's clients were clearly less susceptible to this fashion, as is evidenced by the publication of this third edition of 'Cheap Buildings'. Story continued steadily constructing in the popular *Moderne* tradition until the Revolution and civil war made this wholly impossible. His designs incorporated many historical and regional motifs to give his architecture a noticeably 'Russian' edge. Throwbacks from Russian medieval mansions *(terem)* can be seen in Projects 3 and 18. Slav and Nordic architectural motifs are found in the high-pitched roofs and elaborately decorated ridges. Projects 6, 14, 16 and 18 reference many buildings painted by the Russian artist Nicholas Roerich in his famous 'Architectural Studies' series of 1904–5.

One interesting example of Story's fluidity of style is his 'English House' (Project 22) which presents a very loose interpretation based around the interiors of certain grander English homes of the period, with its smaller rooms arranged around a large, double-height living-room. Further illustrations of this cosmopolitan quality to Story's work can be found in Projects 54 and 55, which are clearly influenced by Moorish architecture, while Project 11 is an attractive Art Nouveau rendition of the Swiss chalet. At the same time he develops a tendency to become self-referential with certain elements – a sure sign of an established style. Projects 8, 11, 15 and 20 carry references to the Moscow Art Nouveau of the 1900s, with its penchant for the capricious window lintel.

By sub-titling this book 'Cheap Buildings', Story really means 'more affordable buildings' as compared with other dwellings of the period. Here he shows a genuine skill in translating Art Nouveau's more extravagant compositional ideas and motifs to the simpler country dacha. He hangs decorative wooden rings over main wall planes, creates shadow-casts over façades, includes ornamental features (Projects 6, 10, 17, 21 and 22), and generally indulges in that playful style of Russian architecture able to produce the multi-coloured onion domes of St Basil's Cathedral in Moscow's Red Square, four hundred years earlier.

Although Art Nouveau relied strongly on the asymmetry of plans, Project 16 shows Story's command of the axial composition. All window and door centrelines are perfectly aligned, but in a way that allows the overall composition to remain asymmetrical. Similarly, Projects 3, 4, 5, 9 and 10 tend toward square-shaped plans, thus giving the structures a sense of solid geometry.

One assumes the accomplished graphics in this book belong to the author, even if several different drawing styles are found. Designs like Project 17 are presented more thoroughly rendered in the Russian *Beaux-Arts* tradition, while others, like Project 5, are depicted in the linear form.

A Sustainable Architecture

Due partly to the period in which he worked, Story's designs demonstrate an inbuilt sustainability. With a few exceptions, locally grown wood served as the primary construction material, and due to the severity of Russia's winters, good insulation was always a strong consideration, with designs tending towards the thicker wall (Projects 19, 20 and 21). Plan variations invariably offer winter options for the more flimsy summer dacha constructions. Although such walls are initially more expensive, they offer the advantage of conserving energy, thus making the structure more comfortable and economical, long term. The fascinating and detailed inclusion of two ice-storage houses (Projects 45 and 46), takes the idea of sustainability further than most would go today.

Options for Projects 8, 10, 13 and 14 demonstrate how a simple wall surface can be inexpensively transformed into something more aesthetic, using patterned bead-board. Project 17 presents the option of insulation in the form of stucco rendering. At the same time it suggests using a higher proportion of sand and gravel to reduce costs.

Like most commercial architects of his time, Story shows a genuine attentiveness to his clients' budget. He frequently offers simpler variations (Projects 1 and 23) or the possibility of building in stages (Projects 12 and 14), in which the second stage is cleverly designed to be erected while living in the first. He also offers the option of leaving the first stage as is, should, one assumes, the money run out.

In a similar vein, designs like Project 5 provide rental options for part of a house to help offset the costs of construction. Likewise, Project 16 suggests a choice of two different versions, one cheap and one more expensive. Project 17 shows an interestingly modern flexibility of design, offering alternative locations for partitions between the dining and living areas, showing an awareness of the increasingly popular open-plan.

As to the costs of each house presented here, it is very hard to render them in today's prices. A Weimar-style inflation of the Russian rouble began in 1917 and the book's author states the reason for this 4th edition as 'financial'. The editor also notes that the prices in this edition had increased by a third since the last printing. By July 1917, during the period of the Provisional Government, the rouble devalued by the same amount as this each week. How many weeks earlier the book had been published is impossible to say. If one crudely guesses that the rouble here had devalued x 2 since it stood at ten to one pound sterling (1915), then multiply by 70 for today's value. That would leave Project No 1 (1000 roubles) costing, £14,000 ($21,000 US).

The Dacha after the Russian Revolution

Although the furious broom of the Revolution swept away most vestiges of the old way of life and many personal dachas were appropriated by the state, the dacha culture itself survived remarkably well into the Soviet era. It remained one of the few areas of life left open to individual expression. The Soviet state, like the monarchy before it, still awarded its citizens free plots of land to build their summer homes. While the land remained state property, for many the Soviet dacha became a *de facto* place of permanent, rent-free living. Because many families still remembered their pre-Revolutionary dacha lifestyle outside the city and surrounded by nature, they attempted to recreate it in *sadovodstvo* (gardening) settlements. The *sadovodstvo* lands were distributed among state employees and the land usually divided into standard rectangular plots of 20 x30 metres (*shest sotok*) or 30x40 metres (*dvenadtsat sotok*). The Soviet dacha gradually evolved as a curious combination of communist egalitarianism blended with the capitalist cult of the individual. Many houses built between 1950 and 1980 were designed and constructed in a more Russian traditional style with patterned windows and bead-board walls. The freedom of self-expression even extended into the realm of religious organisations, some of which were permitted to occupy buildings described as 'dachas'. Novaia Ropsha *sadovodstvo* for example, possessed its own dacha Baptist church, although strictly speaking in contradiction with the Soviet state.

The recent return of capitalism to Russia has produced another boost for the dacha, although some would say lacking in the former skills of craftsmanship and design. Huge dacha-mansions have sprung out of the soil around Moscow and St Petersburg with little planning regulation or a sense of the landscape that they inhabit. Yet the presence of Russian historical design still lingers in many of the surrounding buildings. It is hoped that this book might provide fresh references to these simpler, more economical and ecologically friendly methods of constructing the elegant domestic home.

ANTON GLIKIN 2009

Архитектурное книгоиздательство М. Г. Стракуна.

Петроградъ, Невскій просп., д. № 32. Тел. 165-20.

ДЕШЕВЫЯ
ПОСТРОЙКИ

Дача г. Радугина, Сел. Александровское
Приморской ж. д.

Дачная Архитектура

Альбомъ

проектовъ, домовъ,

дачъ, служебныхъ и

другихъ построекъ.

Выпускъ 2-й.

ИЗДАНІЕ 1-ОЕ.

Вл. Г. СТОРИ.

Талонъ,

предназначенный служить для установленія болѣе тѣсной связи въ сношеніяхъ съ авторомъ по разнаго рода могущимъ возникнуть у читателя вопросамъ, вытекающимъ изъ примѣненія къ практикѣ проектовъ настоящаго изданія.

Съ требованіями обращаться: въ Книгоиздательство М. Г. Стракуна, Петроградъ, Невскій пр., д. № 32. Тел. 165-20.

Architectural Publishing House of M G Strakun
Petrograd Nevsky Prosp, D. No 32 Tel 165-20

CHEAP BUILDINGS

[Drawing] Mr Radugin's Dacha, Alexandrovskoye village, beside the Primorskaya Railway

Dacha Architecture

Album

projects, houses,
dachas, offices
and other buildings

2nd Volume

4th edition

Vl. G. STORY

Voucher,

to be used by the reader for contacting the author regarding any questions that might follow on from the practical application of projects in this edition.

All inquiries to; the **M G Strakun** Publishing House,
Petrograd, Nevsky Pr, House No 32. Tel 165-20

From the Author

For many years now the author has been collecting design materials in order to print several editions of works such as those found in this album. As the amount has increased considerably, this album is now being published to follow directly on from the second and third editions.

Owing partly to the above considerations and partly for financial reasons, this album of 'cheap buildings' now includes 75 projects from the second edition, while another 40 projects will soon be printed in a separate edition. All the texts here are original and completely revised. The informational sections try to answer the many questions received from private clients. Additionally the author has added many new architectural and stylistic facts and included a number of clarifying drawings and statistics.

As a result this edition has evolved into more of an informational brochure, making it far more practical than those previous, especially for customers with specific questions.

In the light of this the author hopes very much that, as in previous years, his esteemed clients will not abandon him and continue to send their queries and also valuable pointers to any drawbacks they have found. For their counsel, the author is always deeply grateful.

1917   Vl. Story

From the Editor

Due to the pressures at this time of war, it has been very difficult to procure the paper and organise the printing of this edition. So, with permission from the author the editor has changed slightly the original text and layout to save space. As a result this volume has assumed the character of a self-teaching manual for building art. Additionally small changes have been made to some statistics relating to individual project, which the author then re-checked before this edition was printed. The price of buildings listed here are one-third higher than those of the previous edition.

1917   M. Strakun

The Architectural Construction Office
of the building technician

V. G. Story.

who accepts orders for:
Projects, estimates, detailed drawings, and adaption of existing projects.

At the client's request we can offer: technical observation during construction; assistance in obtaining bank credits; construction of houses, rental houses and workshops.

Construction and financial consulting

Architectural projects starting from 35 roubles

We have a wide variety of completed projects that include wooden and stone houses and dachas. They range from the cheap to the expensive, covering the needs of a wide range of the population. We offer fast completion and a courteous service at affordable prices.

Please contact us either by post, or in person

Petrograd, Nevsky Prospect, 32

Project No 1

Because of its small size this house is best set on stone pillars. The recommended sizes for these are:

a) Corner pillars – width 0.33, length 0.33, depth 0.33.

b) Internal pillars – width 0.25, length 0.25, depth 0.33.

The distance between columns and the centre should be no more than 1.5 sazhens (to prevent curvature). For simpler construction the rooms should be built in sequence.

The price of this building starts at:

600 roubles - wood siding with vertical supports, with one Russian fireplace and a tar-paper roof.

1000 roubles - tinned roof timber.

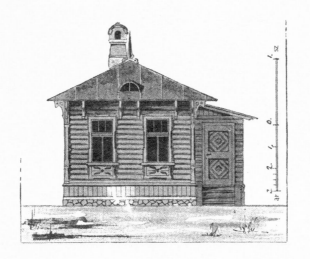

PROJECT No 1

Area 2 x 3 sz

Price from **1000** rbls

PLAN

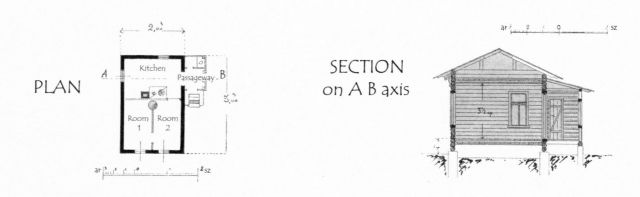

SECTION
on A B axis

PLAN
VARIATION

Project No 2

Fantasy House.

    Total area – 2x3 sazhens. The design includes two cold rooms at the building's rear. It also includes two similar cold rooms on the second floor. Very comfortable as a summertime dacha, it can also be used in winter as a hunter's cabin.

PROJECT No 2

Winter Area	. .	2×3
Total Area . .	.	$4{,}60 \times 4{,}60$
Price, winter area	.	**1000** rbls
Total price	. .	**2000** rbls

CROSS-SECTION

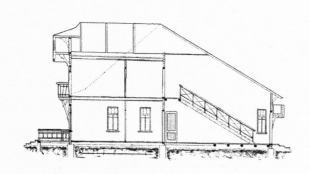

PLAN

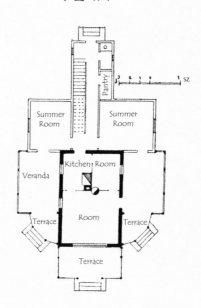

Project No 3

To create a warmer floor at ground level we recommend setting the house on flat foundations at a height of 0.33 sz, or the equivalent of 2.5 brick slabs. This protects it from under-earth freezing. Please note that in this project and all others in this book we use the same standard foundations.

For a more effective terrace it is better to leave the roof beams open. For a lighter-weight project we recommend using the more flexible blue spruce timber.

PROJECT No 3

Area 3 x 3 sz

Price from **1500** rbls

SECTION on BA Axis

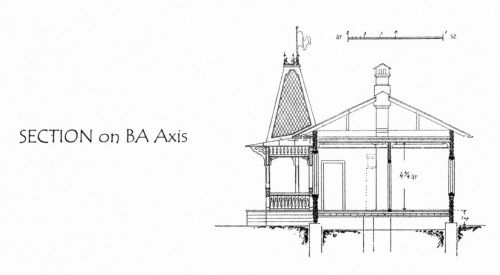

PLAN

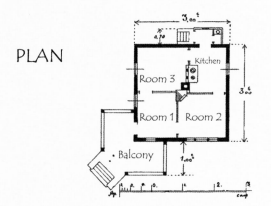

PLAN
VARIATION

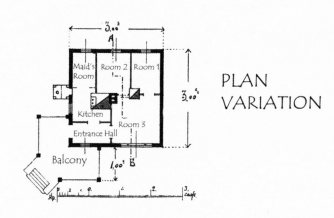

Project No 4

The external cladding is made from a 1 duim, single-layered, wood planking. This type of house is best suited for summer use. 2.5 duim and 2 duim wooden planks, supported by principal posts embedded into the necking, are recommended for the columns. If a lighter construction option is chosen, the price reduces by 30%.

The side terraces can be made more effectively by substituting concrete with doubled-up wood planking, set at a height of 0.25 duim to allow for water drainage.

PROJECT No 4

Area 3 x 3 sz

Price from **1900** rbls

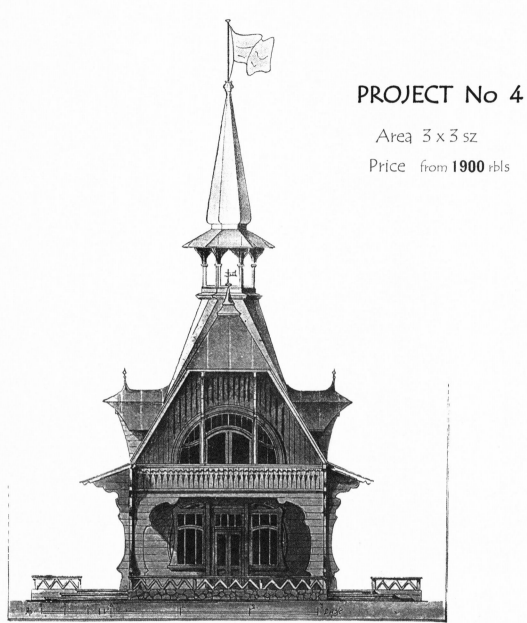

1st Floor PLAN   2nd Floor PLAN   CROSS-SECTION

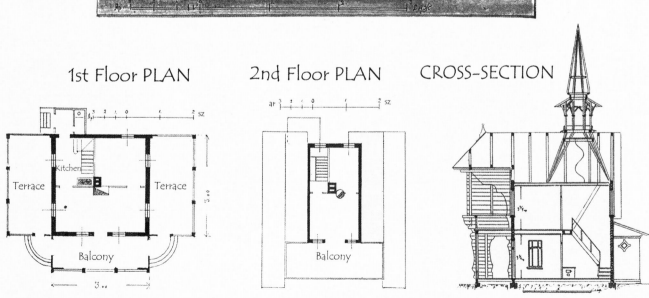

Terrace

Kitchen

Terrace

Balcony

Balcony

Project No 5

We offer a basement option for this house, dug to a depth of 1 arshin. If this is chosen, the house will be without foundations and set instead on columns at a two plank distance. All the basement walls must be constructed out of doubled-up planks. This basement can be used for chickens, dry wood or food storage. Its entrance will be from the yard. The above option would prove cheaper and more effective than constructing a separate storage building. We offer three plan options. One contains two separate flats of two rooms, including separate kitchens, entrances and a terrace. Wooden steps and storage space would be placed on either side of the building. It is also possible to add another floor to the existing plan (for either winter or summer use).

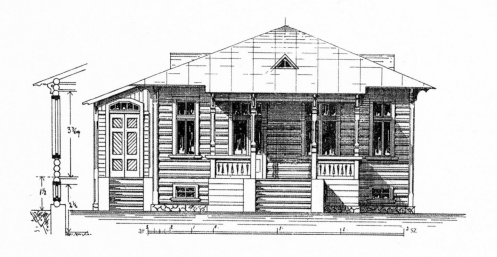

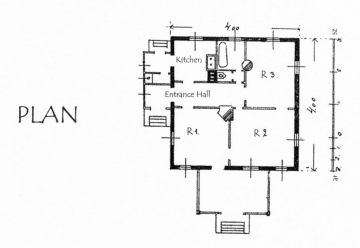

PLAN

PROJECT No 5

Area 4 x 4 sz

Price from 2000 rbls

2nd PLAN VARIATION

PLAN VARIATION

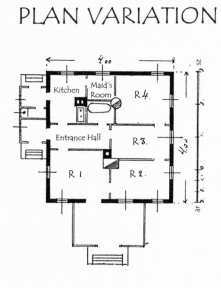

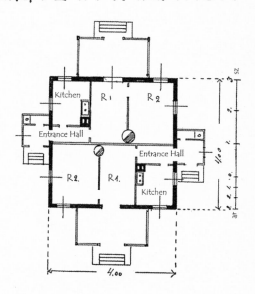

Project No 6

A 3x4 sazhens log house with a 2x3 sazhens lower wing, suitable for a large family. Stairs lead up from the dining room. The maid's room could also be a bathroom. The roof is wood planking, but could also be made from a similar quantity of logs –15 square sazhens. For this option you would require 3 logs, 4 sazhens long, set securely into the walls.

PROJECT No 6.

Area 4 x 5 sz

Price from 3600 rbls

2nd Floor PLAN

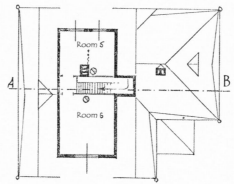

1st Floor PLAN

SECTION on AB axis

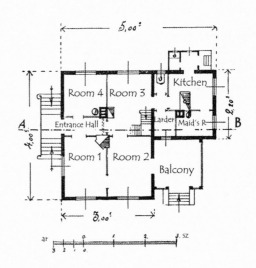

Project No 7

Single-floor beamed house with inside bathroom. A columned pergola veranda with sheet-metal roof stands above one corner. The stairs (not shown in the plan) can be located at any part of the veranda. The house itself is best set just above the ground on columns.

PROJECT No 7

Area 5,33×4,00 sz

Price from **4300** rbls

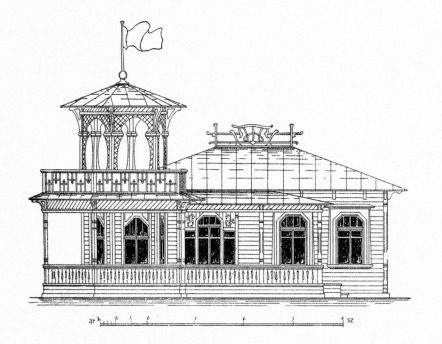

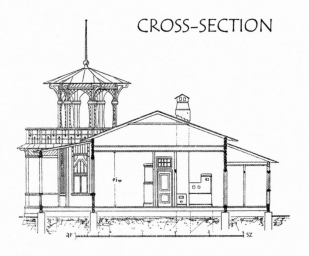

CROSS-SECTION

PLAN

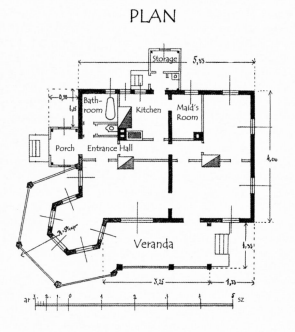

Storage

5,33

Bath-room

Kitchen

Maid's Room

Porch

Entrance Hall

Veranda

Project No 8

Several variations are possible for this project. The overall size can differ by 9 square sazhens of log walling – added or subtracted.

PROJECT No 8

Area 3 x 4 sz

Price from **2900** rbls

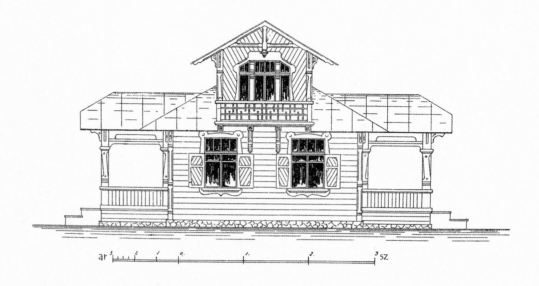

PLAN

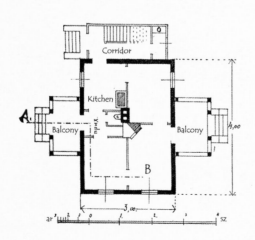

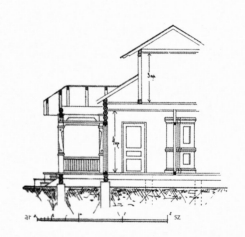

SECTION on AB axis

Project No 9

Two-storey house with two balconies, one enclosed on the ground floor. It features ornamental wood planking under the eaves.

1st Floor

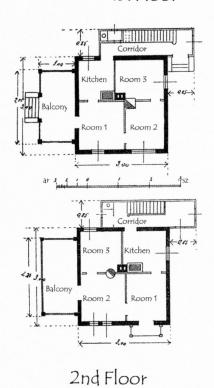

2nd Floor

PROJECT No 9

Area 3 x 3 sz

Price from **2900** rbls

FACADE

Project No 10

We recommend making the central chimney double-core, one of which will serve as a ventilation pipe drawing from a hole in the concrete foundations. This should be either concrete or ceramic, and if concrete, sealed with tar.

Normally, this kind of design feature is rarely used, but from experience I have found it can provide excellent air circulation and also remove odours from the house. I suggest using this kind of ventilation in all cases where the toilet is located close to the central chimney.

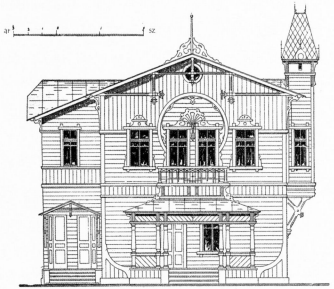

PROJECT No 10

Area 4 x 4 sz

Price from **5300** rbls

CROSS-SECTION

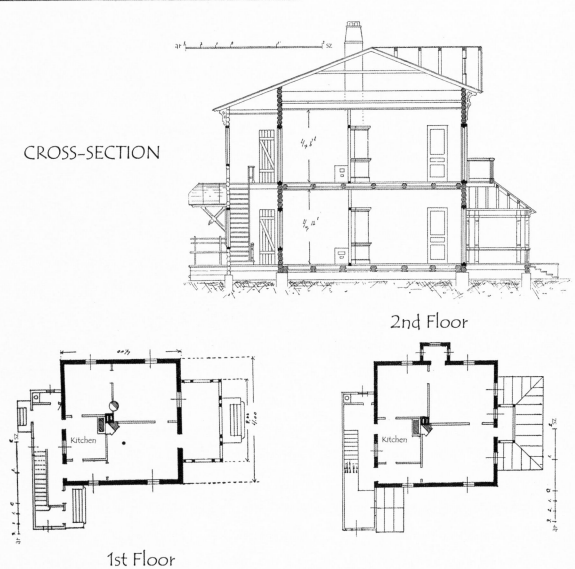

2nd Floor

Kitchen

Kitchen

1st Floor

Project No 11

Swiss-style open beam house. The entrance corridor is divided to provide access to both levels of the building. The second floor is decorated with carved wooden facades which serve as part of an enclosed balcony. To save money, this could be left open-beamed. The external entrance doors are made from a double-thick wood planking.

The project variation offers a ground floor area of 5x3 sazhens and an upstairs of 3x3 sazhens. Here we would suggest the inclusion of a bathroom and water closet - not shown on the plan as there is little difference in price with or without. Overall, the plan variation would require an extra 3 sq sazhens for the floor and ceiling areas; 6 sq sazhens for the walls, 4 sq sazhens for the roof and 0.20 square sazhens for the foundation. The approximate price is between 3200 and 4600 roubles. Also, the second floor could be enlarged to 3x4 sazhens if the first floor is expanded correspondingly.

PROJECT No 11

Area 3 x 4 sz

Price from **2700** rbls

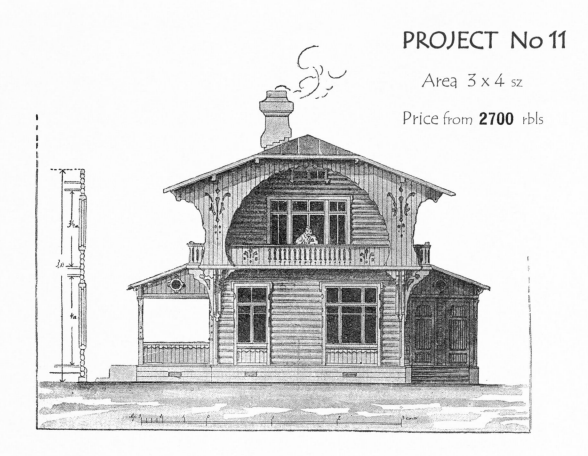

1st Floor

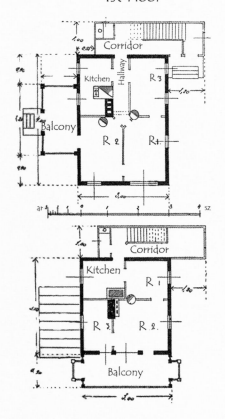

2nd Floor

Variation for Project No 11

Area 3 x 5 sz

Price from **3200** rbls

1st Floor

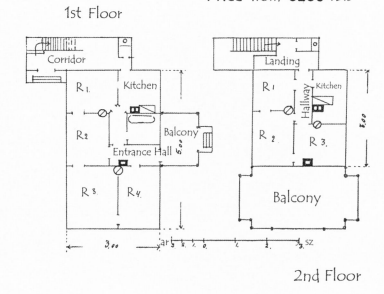

2nd Floor

Project No 12

Here we offer a building for construction over a period of several years. The first year would create a single floor house with a pergola (summer or winter), two rooms and an outside corridor. A second stage could then be added without involving any demolition of the existing house - creating a building of two additional floors. The stairs to the pergola can be extended up to the second floor. The plan for the second stage's second floor would be identical to that of the ground floor. Water closets can be installed in the bathrooms.

The first stage cost is 2000-2700 roubles; the second stage is 2900-4000 roubles.

PROJECT No 12

Area 3 x 4 + 3 x 4 sz
Construction in two stages
Price   1st stage   from   **2000** rbls
»   2nd   »   »   **2900** rbls

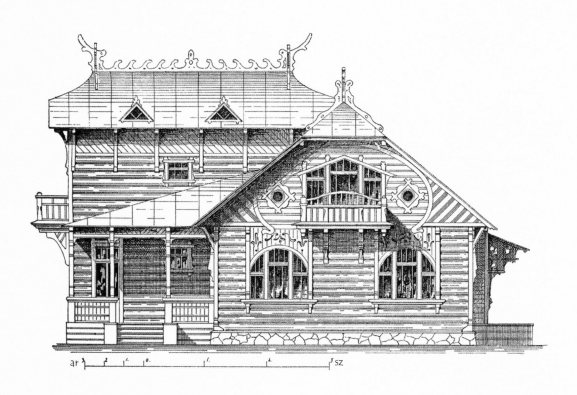

ar 3   2   1   0.   1   2   3 SZ

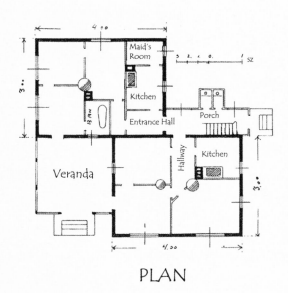

PLAN

Project No 13

A building partitioned into two flats of different sizes. The upper section of the larger flat (3x3) is a completely separate room, but the upper section of the smaller flat can only be used as a one room pergola in summer. However, if constructed from wooden logs it could also become habitable in winter. Metal beams should be installed under the stove areas of the kitchens with the ventilation pipes beside them. The uppermost section of the building is glazed on three sides (9 square sazhens of glass). This can be a summer gallery. If double-glazed it could also be used in winter as, say, a photographer's or artist's studio. The external walls could also be rendered. To estimate the cost of rendering, calculate the total wall area but omit the summer gallery which must be of wood only.

PROJECT No 13

Area 3 x 5 sz
Price from **3300** rbls

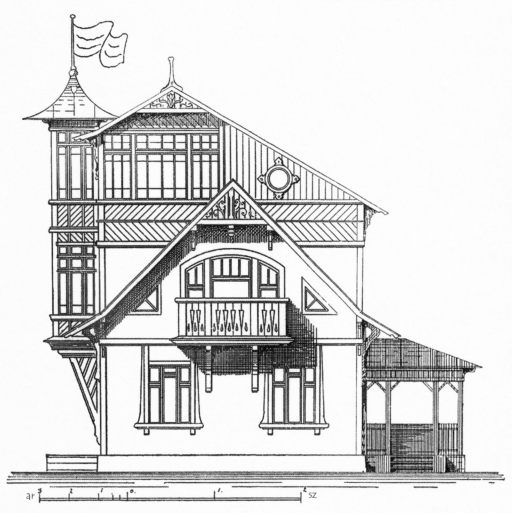

ar 3   2   1   0.   1.   2 sz

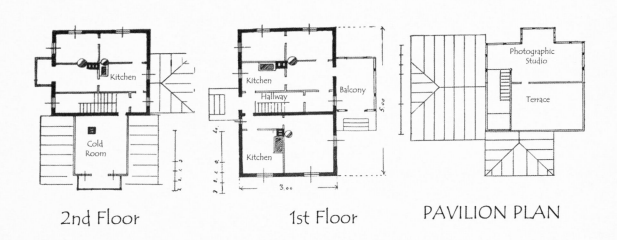

2nd Floor   1st Floor   PAVILION PLAN

Project No 14

This project can be completed in three stages: each is designed so as not to interfere with the previous stage.

The plan shows this building as 36.80 square sazhens – here outlined in black. The external walls can be made from 2.5 wooden planks to create a summer house, or from logs to allow winter use. The oven in the kitchen should be installed close to the central chimney.

To join the downstairs apartments together, door 'a' can be created and one of the kitchens removed. In addition, one of the water closets could be used as a storage area.

The estimate contains four balconies, each one 4 sazhens long. Three of these could be halved in size to add more indoor space.

PROJECT No 14

Area

$3 \times 4 + 3 \times 4$

Construction in three stages

Price
1st stage from **2100** rbls

2nd stage from **1700** rbls

3rd stage (veranda) from **1200** rbls

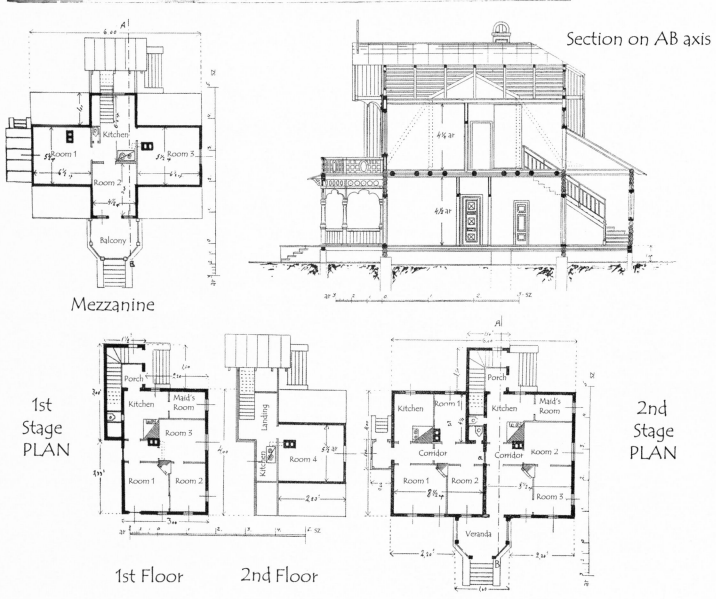

Mezzanine

Section on AB axis

1st Stage PLAN

2nd Stage PLAN

1st Floor

2nd Floor

Project No 15

Norwegian-style house. One variation is to construct the entire upper part of this house from wooden planks. Storage space is placed under the kitchen with trap-door access from the corridor. The columns in the same storage area of the plan are shown as sufficient to support the inside walls. The kitchen contains a Russian oven. It should be remembered that Russian ovens must always be set on their own special foundations and close to a chimney. Owing to their weight, installation of Russian ovens directly on top of wooden beams is not recommended. It is also forbidden by Russian law.

PROJECT
No 15

Area

5,20×7,30 SZ

Price from

8000 rbls

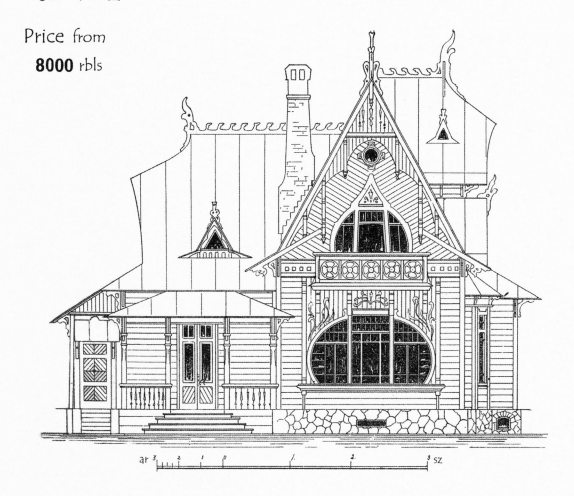

ar 3 2 1 0 1. 2. 3 SZ

PROJECT No 15

1st Floor PLAN

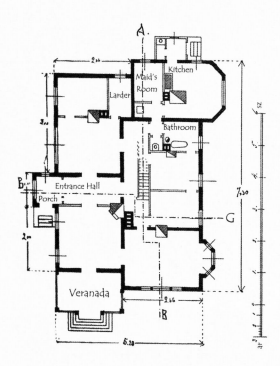

Kitchen

Maid's Room

Larder

Bathroom

Entrance Hall

Porch

Veranada

2nd Floor PLAN

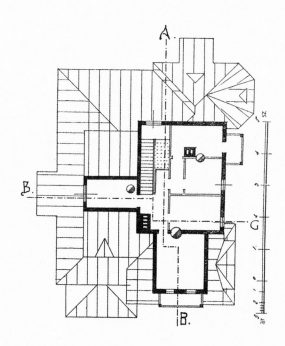

SECTION on BG Axis

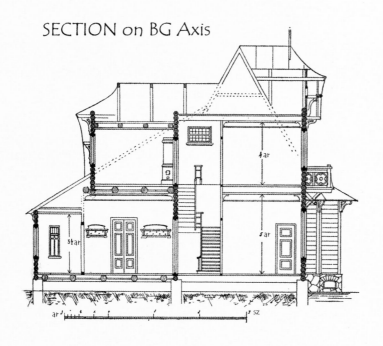

PROJECT
No 15

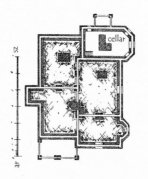

BASEMENT PLAN

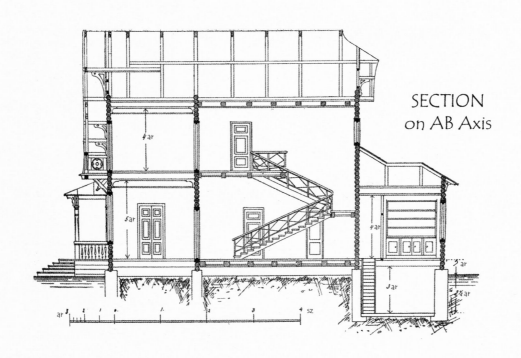

SECTION
on AB Axis

Project No 16

A dacha-mansion. Its external walls are made either from a high-quality lining-board or, alternatively, plank-siding. The wall spaces above the windows are decorated with laquer paint and ornamental design. The upper section of the house is a self-contained flat with a small kitchen separated from the room behind. The access stairs to the ground floor are isolated by a partition wall. An economy version of this house would involve constructing it entirely out of wood planking, which is cheaper.

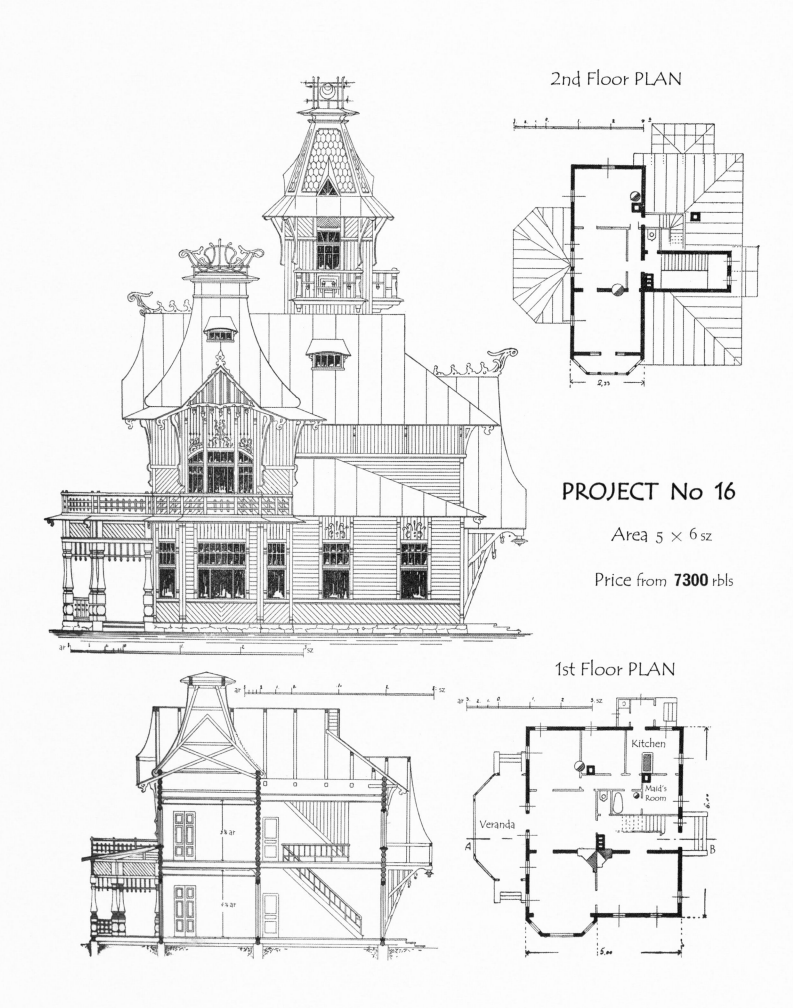

2nd Floor PLAN

PROJECT No 16

Area 5 × 6 sz

Price from **7300** rbls

1st Floor PLAN

Kitchen

Maid's Room

Veranda

A

B

Project No 17

Dacha-mansion. The external walls can be finished with a single layer of high-quality wood planking. If a sturdier construction is required, sand-rendering should be used - a preferable technique to ordinary rendering. We suggest all wooden surfaces are painted dark red and the sand-rendered surfaces white – to give a more effective contrast. A sliding partition is set between the living and dining-rooms to provide a possible larger space to be used for dancing or home theatre etc.

PROJECT No 17

Area 5 x 6

Price from **6900** rbls

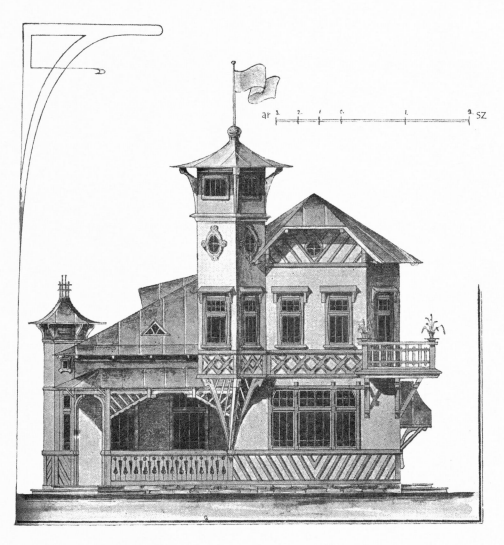

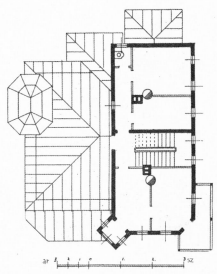

1st Floor PLAN

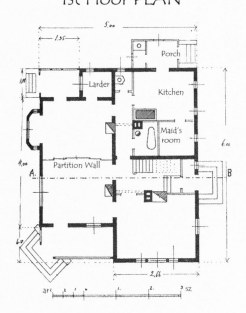

Porch

Larder

Kitchen

Maid's room

Partition Wall

A.

B

SECTION on AB Axis

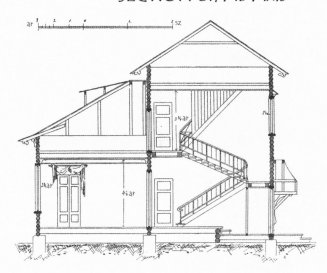

Project No 18

Norwegian-style. This house stands on a single foundation. The space next to the water-closet on the second floor can be used for a staircase up to the turret room. The ground and second floor galleries are glazed (about 26 square sazhens of glass).

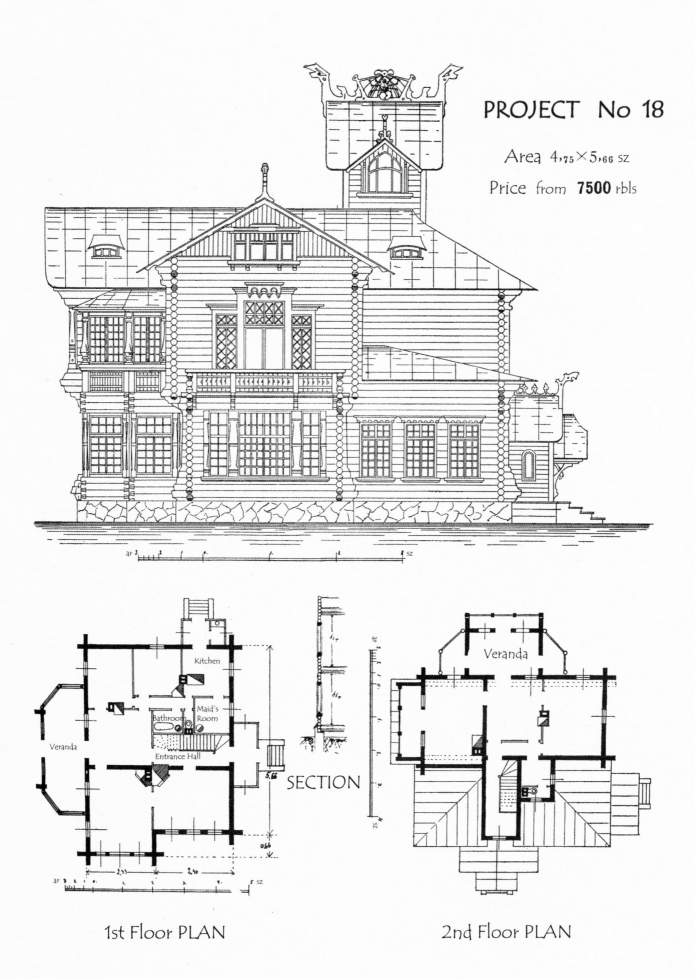

PROJECT No 18

Area 4,75 × 5,66 sz

Price from **7500** rbls

Veranda

Kitchen

Bathroom

Maid's Room

Entrance Hall

SECTION

Veranda

1st Floor PLAN

2nd Floor PLAN

Project No 19

A French-style, stone dacha-mansion. All external walls are rendered and have brick cornices. The beams are metal: 8 in the ground floor, 7 in the second floor. The stairs are ceramic and mounted on metal supports. The landings are concrete and the roof is tiled. The top floor room can house a water tank large enough to supply the whole house.

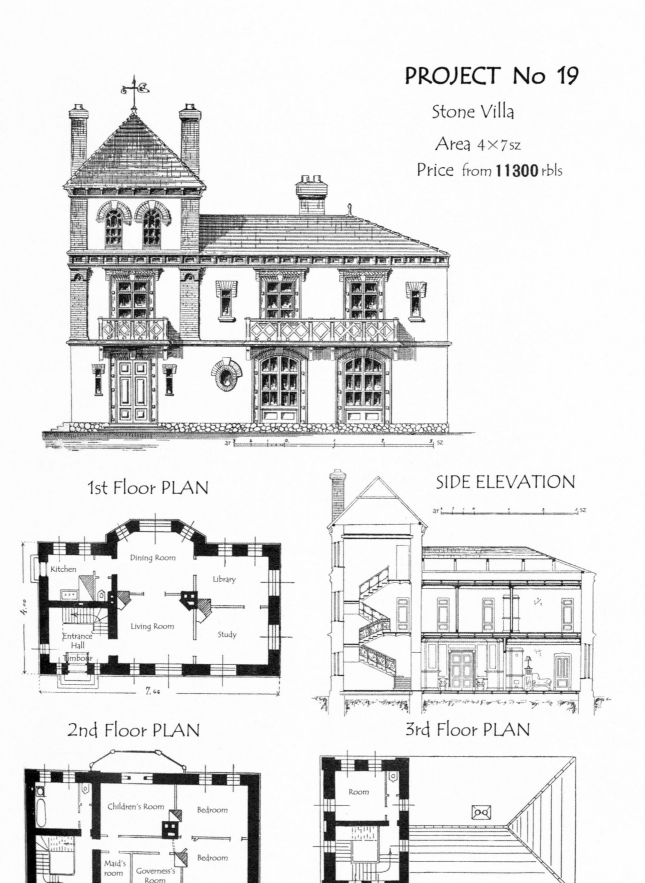

PROJECT No 19

Stone Villa

Area 4×7 sz

Price from **11300** rbls

1st Floor PLAN

Kitchen
Dining Room
Library
Living Room
Study
Entrance Hall
Tambour

SIDE ELEVATION

2nd Floor PLAN

Children's Room
Bedroom
Maid's room
Governess's Room
Bedroom

3rd Floor PLAN

Room

Project No 20

'Modern' style, stone dacha-mansion. The second floor walls, A and B, are log (6.22 square sazhens), covered with a single layer (1 duim thick) of wood panelling, then rendered. All window cornices are made from brick, some are designed for water drainage, some decoration. In this building it is easy to interchange room functions. The structure contains metal 'I' beams (7 duims width).

All walls, internal and external are designed with niches to accommodate cabinets - either for food storage (external), or books or clothes (internal).

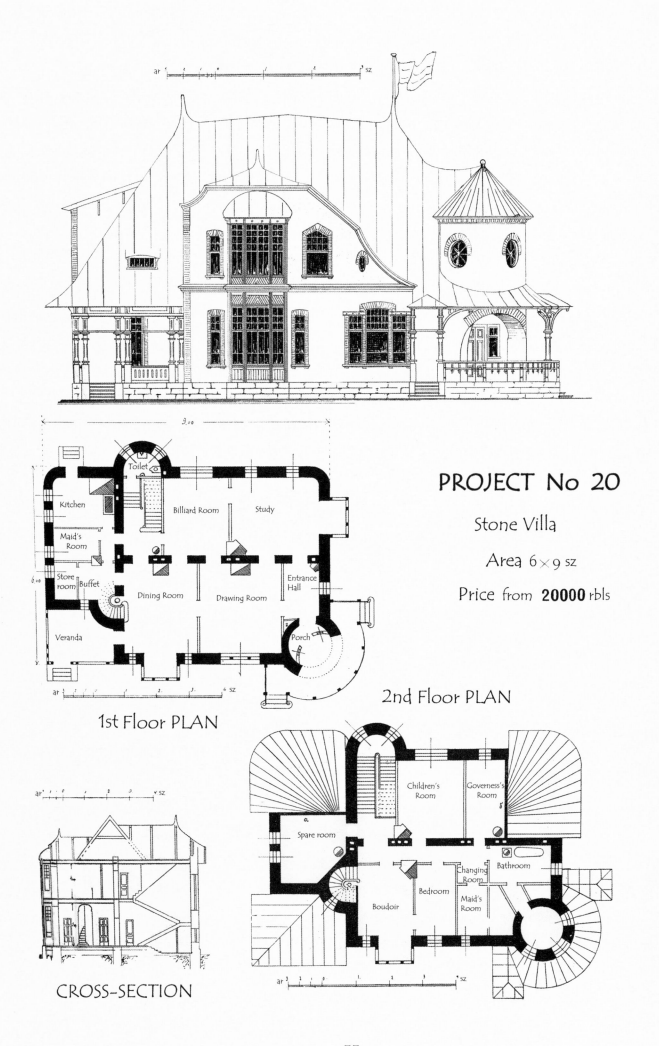

PROJECT No 20

Stone Villa

Area 6×9 sz

Price from **20000** rbls

1st Floor PLAN

Kitchen

Billiard Room

Study

Maid's Room

Store room | Buffet

Dining Room

Drawing Room

Entrance Hall

Veranda

Porch

Toilet

2nd Floor PLAN

Children's Room

Governess's Room

Spare room

Bathroom

Changing Room

Boudoir

Bedroom

Maid's Room

CROSS-SECTION

Project No 21

    This house is built on a natural stone foundation and employs brick cladding on each of the ground floor corners: base width 0.40 sazhen, (3 bricks lengthwise). This brick cladding should use a cement mortar. The ground floor interior walls are stone, finished with a single layer of bricks to be set in alternate vertical and horizontal lines. The external walls are cavitied for insulation – helping to warm the house in winter. Without this design feature (see detail) the house would be uninhabitable.

    If the landscape is suitable, a basement of about 16 square sazhens can be set within a section of the foundations. This basement floor can be left as bare earth or covered with decking. The basement ceiling should be arched and made from concrete or brick, supported by metal beams (8 duims width). The second floor internal walls are unrendered. On one side of the house they will extend down to the ground floor. The lower part of the turret can be used as a pergola. This project is an example of a building that:

    a) can use a basement floor as a living area
    b) uses natural stone in construction
    c) utilises the shapes of the local landscape to its advantage
    d) comes in a wide variety of sizes

    In this project water pipes can also be set within the basement floor.

PROJECT No 21

Stone and Wooden House
Area 6×7,₅₀ sz
Price: Lower, stone section **11.300** rbls
Upper, wood section from **4.700** rbls

CROSS-SECTION

PROJECT No 21

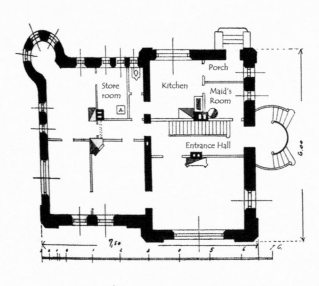

1st Floor PLAN

BASEMENT PLAN

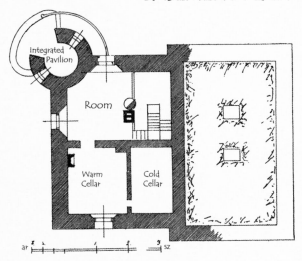

Integrated Pavilion

Room

Warm Cellar

Cold Cellar

ar | | | | sz

2nd Floor PLAN

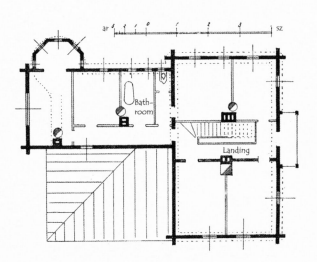

ar | | | | sz

Bath-room

Landing

Detail, Interior Wall Finish

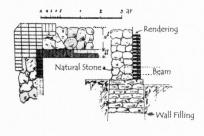

ar

Rendering

Natural Stone

Beam

Wall Filling

SECTION

Project No 22

English-style house. In some western countries a new kind of hygienic house is being designed, specifically for single family use. Much of everyday family life is accommodated within a main living room with good ventilation - the largest single space in the house. This large room can also be used as a children's play area, a winter garden, a space to entertain visitors, as well as for dining, family concerts, etc.

This building is a good demonstration of this new living-style. To make the project more economical we could replace the main room's varied lighting units with a central fixture. The main room is one and a half storeys high with its walls constructed out of stone. The house's front entrance leads directly from the central façade and is flanked by terraces. Smaller rooms are set on either side of the large central room - to be used for living, guests, dining, work, etc. The servants' quarters are housed in the rear of the building along with the store rooms. Above the central room on the first floor, a corridor system leads to the bedrooms and a terrace. The central room is 12.5 square sazhens – with 28 cubic sazhens of open space. During the day this room can be used as a meeting room for the whole family. In the evenings it can accommodate a considerable number of people. Bookshelves, paintings or collections can be placed in the corridors around this room. It can also be used as a home-theatre or for family concerts, etc.

Because the bedrooms are all upstairs it gives them a less cramped feel. An ice room and basement storage can be built under the servants' rooms at the rear of the house.

PROJECT No 22

ENGLISH STYLE HOUSE

Area $6{,}66 \times 8{,}66$ sz

Price from **16.000** rbls

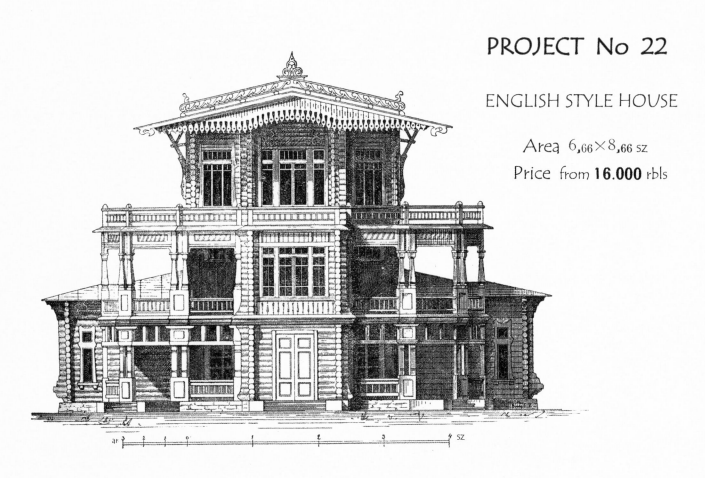

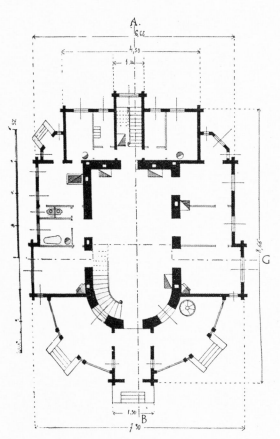

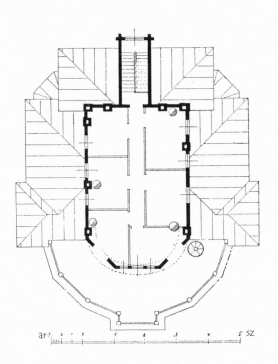

1st Floor PLAN   2nd Floor PLAN

PROJECT No 22

SECTION on BG Axis

PROJECT No 22

SECTION on AB Axis

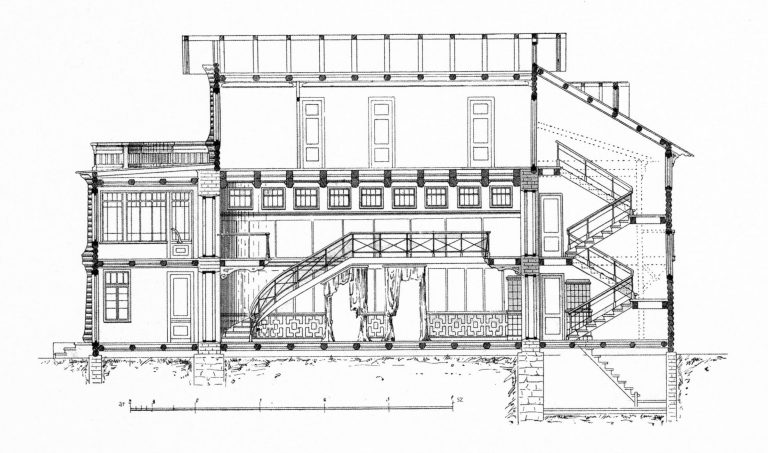

DRAFT
PROJECTS

The following motifs
are here to stimulate
ideas for different
plans and facades.
In some cases you can
make new plan variations
from these examples.

Project No 23

A small house with many facilities, including bathroom and warm-water closet. The ground floor has been raised by 2 arshins to create space for a basement. Its height will depend on the type desired – either for food storage, wood storage, chickens, etc. If the basement walls are log (see explanation for project No 5) its depth could be extended by up to 3.5 arshins. This space could then be used by servants or for rental – when it would operate as a separate space.

Project No 24

Small family dacha. All rooms are large. The office size can be easily enlarged by moving the servant's room to the existing bathroom and separating the pantry from the kitchen. If necessary, a mezzanine can be added upstairs.

PROJECT No 23

Area 3x4 sz

Price from **2400** rbls

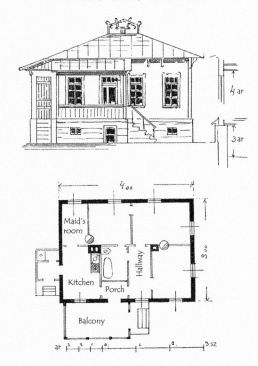

PROJECT No 24

Area 5x5 sz

Price from **4000** rbls

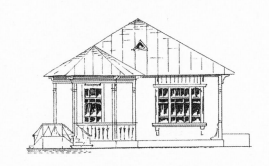

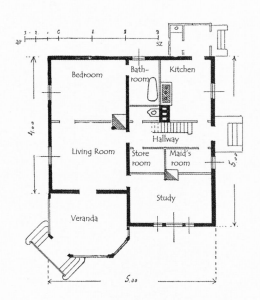

Project No 25

Ground floor area of 4x5 sazhens with partition walls. The house has four rooms and a bathroom. The upper floor (4x3 sazhens) has a separate entrance and contains three warm rooms and a kitchen. The fourth room can be cold - when finished in wooden planks or stone; or warm (habitable in winter) - when made out of logs.

PROJECT No 25

Area 4 x 5 sz

Price from **4000** rbls

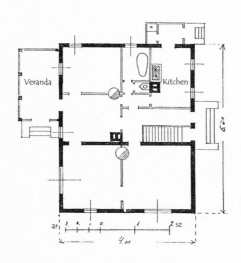

1st Floor PLAN

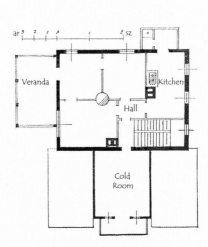

2nd Floor PLAN

Project No 26

The plan shows this building's upper floor as a summer house only, but it could also be used in winter, depending on the wall materials chosen. In the latter case, the thin partition walls must be replaced by 24 square sazhens of thicker walling. Above this is access to an upper rounded balcony topped by a flag-pole. This house would fit well on a river bank or beside the sea.

Project No 27

House with brick ground floor (3x3 sazhens) and terrace, plus stairs leading to the upper floors. The terrace and staircase have supporting brick columns. This technique allows upper floors to be larger than the ground floor.

PROJECT No 26

Area 4 x 4 sz

Price from **3200** rbls

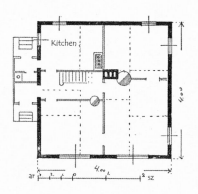

PROJECT No 27

Area 3 x 3 or 3 x 5 sz

Price from **3600** rbls

1st Floor PLAN

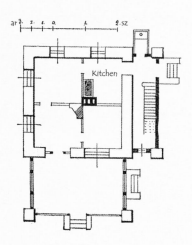

2nd Floor PLAN

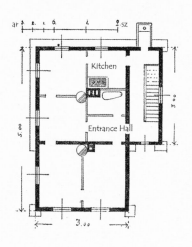

Project No 28

A special project to create two separate rental flats. A bathroom or toilet can be built under the staircase of the ground floor. The first and second floor plans are separate units but share a common entrance.

Plan variation – four room flat with bathroom giving the option of renting each room separately. The price will be the same for all plan variations as they only require the addition of partitions. In each option the wall is 5 sazhens long. Some plans are presented without partitions. The ground floor beams are 4 sazhens long and should be fixed within the external walls. In some variations the water-closet can also be within the bathroom.

PROJECT No 28

Area 4 x 5 sz

Price from 5300 rbls

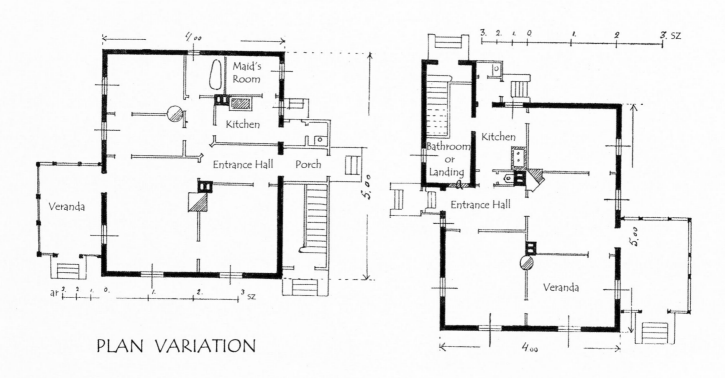

PLAN VARIATION

1st and 2nd Floor PLAN

Project No 29

Rental house. This building can be either stuccoed or given a plank siding. Each floor contains two separate flats with two entrances. They are served by a single staircase encased in a stone wall that is part exterior. All flats have the same area and layout downstairs and upstairs. Each room possesses its own entrance to enable individual rental. If the ground around the foundations permits, the building can be raised one arshin and a basement added to create additional small rooms for rental.

Project No 30

House for cheap rental rooms with a communal kitchen. This design allows for another floor to be added with the staircase set on one of the terraces. A 1.5 arshin basement could also be dug as in Project 29, to make one large kitchen, bathroom, servants' room and storage room.

PROJECT No 29

Rental House

Area 6 x 8 sz

Price from **10.700** rbls

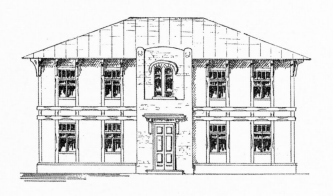

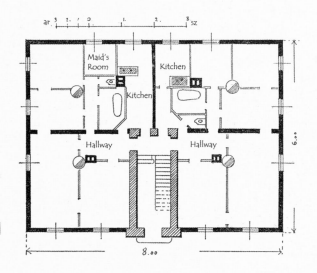

PROJECT No 30

House with Cheap Rooms

Area 4 x 6 sz

Price from **3700** rbls

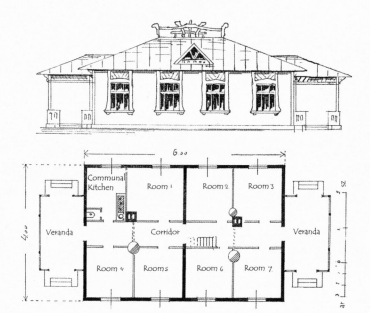

Project No 31

This design is for a small summer dacha or a winter house accommodating a small family. The walls are constructed out of wooden logs. The plan shows an open terrace, but it could also be glazed. This is the cheapest project on offer - after Project No 1.

Project No 32

Design for a house built over several years in three separate stages. The first section is constructed from logs 4 sazhens long and covered with a light roofing.

The second stage will be built separately, with no connection to the first. The final stage will link the two together. The building contains an upper floor able to be either a winter or summer house. A winter house would require an additional 18 square sazhens of wood. Another option is to construct the middle section first, followed by the two outer parts. Large windows could be placed in the rear to add light into the mid-section. The design of the upper floor is identical to the floor below. Terraces, either cold or warm, can be added depending upon the client's wishes.

PROJECT No 31

Area 3 x 3 sz

Price from **1500** rbls

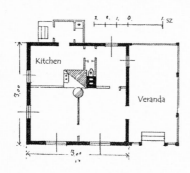

PROJECT No 32

RENTAL HOUSE

Area $2\times3+2\times3+3\times3$ sz

For Construction in Three Stages

Price	1st	Stage	from **700** rbls
	2nd	»	» **800** rbls
	3rd	»	» **1600** rbls

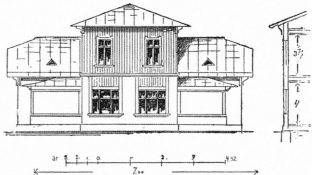

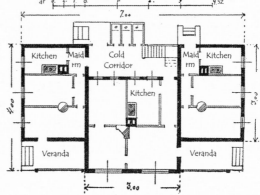

Project No 33

Rental House - exterior rendered with wood column supports. The ground floor contains four shops and two flats with separate entrances. The flats can be divided into two parts (one room plus kitchen). They could also be connected to the shops. The first floor contains three flats, two of three rooms, one with five rooms. All flats have two entrances. These entrances are fed by two separate staircases. This house works well when placed on the corner of a smaller street. In flat No 5 the servants' room can be redesigned as a bathroom.

PROJECT No 33

RENTAL HOUSE

Area $5{,}5 \times 12{,}_{00}$ SZ

Price from **19,300** rbls

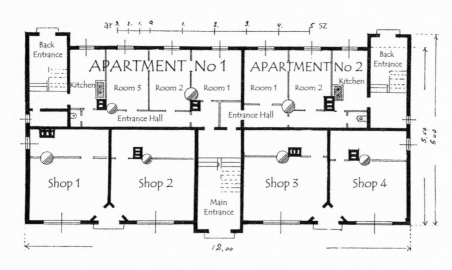

1st Floor PLAN

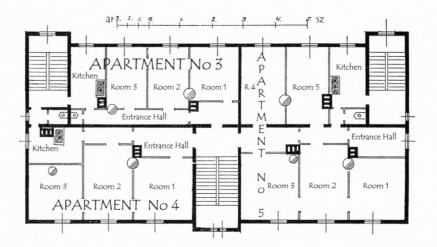

2nd Floor PLAN

UTILITY BUILDINGS

Toilets
Laundry Buildings
Baths
Cow Sheds
Stables
Barns
Poultry Houses
Greenhouses
Swimming Houses
Ice Houses

Project No 34

Outbuilding.

     The ground floor is divided into two halves. One side contains a poultry house (with separate entrance), a stable for one horse, one cow and a cowherd. The other side contains a public bath, laundry and staircase leading to the floor above.

     The top floor contains a two-room servants' flat. Laundry can be dried in a special area directly under the roof. The building's façade design can also be used for a family house, but would require a different interior layout.

PROJECT No 34

Stable, Laundry Room and Servants Quarters

Area 4×6 sz
Price from **4000** rbls

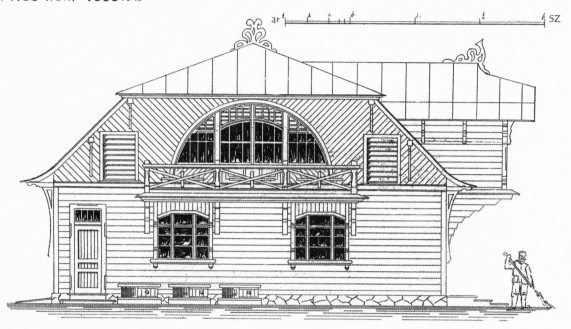

1st Floor PLAN

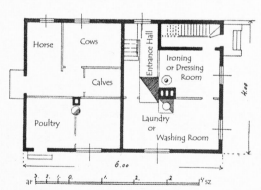

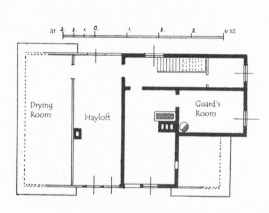

2nd Floor PLAN

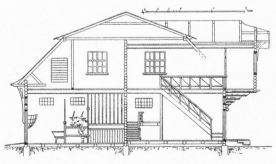

CROSS-SECTION

Project No 35

Semi-detached house.

This rental house is well suited for a small plot of land. It is meant to adjoin the landlord's house and contains a concierge's room. The concierge can service the whole building. The first floor could also house a communal kitchen.

The party-wall must be fire resistant - with a minimum width of 2.5 bricks.

PROJECT No 35

Rental House with Concierge

Area 3×6 sz

Price from **3300** rbls

FACADE
and
SECTION

2nd Floor PLAN

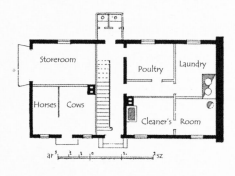

1st Floor PLAN

Project No 36

Multipurpose outbuilding – to include a worker's room, milk room, bath and laundry room.

The first floor contains a laundry drying space accessed by an external staircase. This area is also fronted by removable louvred panels. The eaves should extend out beyond the edge of the drying area.

The façade of this building could also be used for a simple family house.

Project No 37

Stables and storage.

This space is divided by a partition (for reasons of hygiene). The floor in the storage area should be earth. The stable contains a trough. Hay can be stored directly under the roof.

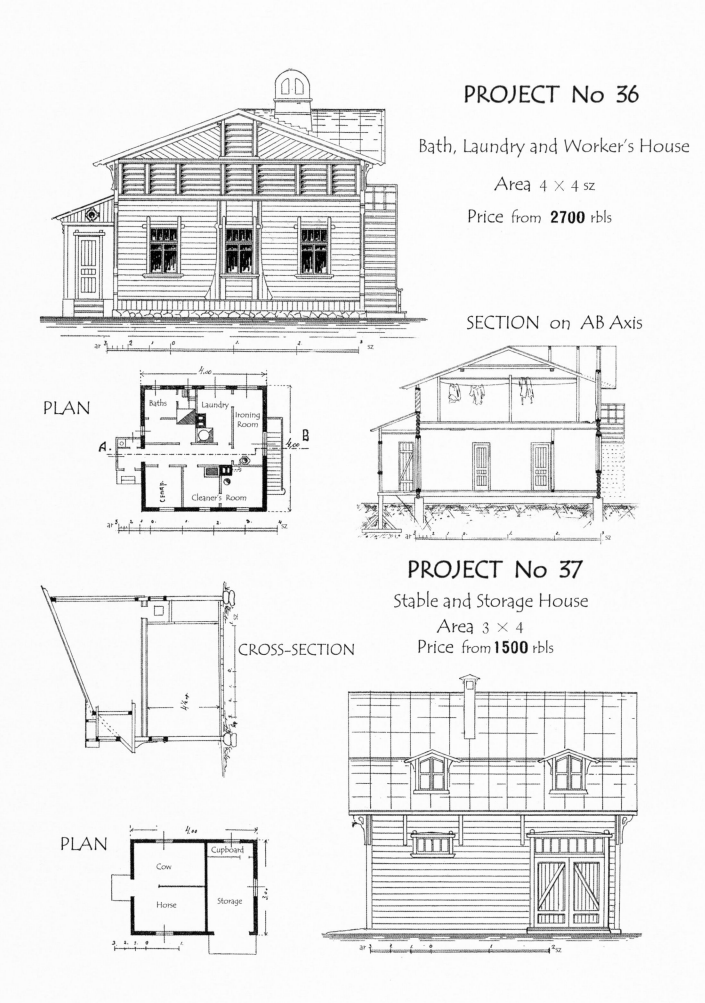

PROJECT No 36

Bath, Laundry and Worker's House

Area 4 × 4 sz

Price from **2700** rbls

SECTION on AB Axis

PLAN

Baths   Laundry   Ironing Room

A.   B

Cleaner's Room

CROSS-SECTION

PROJECT No 37

Stable and Storage House

Area 3 × 4

Price from **1500** rbls

PLAN

Cupboard

Cow

Horse   Storage

Project No 38

Stable, carriage, and poultry house.

The stable entrance contains a built-in hay storage area. The floor is wood panelled, set on a concrete base. The floor has a system of guttering connecting directly to the sewage system. The poultry house floor has a double layer of mastic but can also be concrete. The carriage house floor is earth. All ceilings are double layered and their surfaces treated with mastic. The roof space also contains an area for hay storage.

The stable entrance is covered with a canopy - a good place for cleaning the horse in summer.

Project No 39

Stable with storage.

To economise, this building is made solely from wood planking. The roof space can be used for hay storage and the floor can be either earth or concrete.

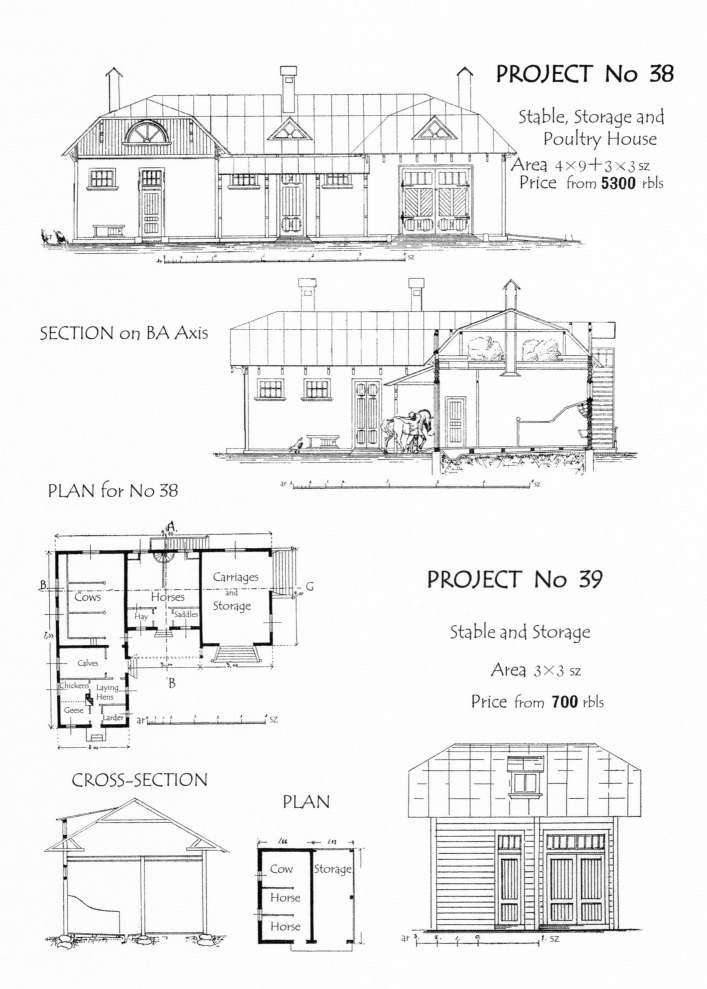

PROJECT No 38

Stable, Storage and
Poultry House
Area 4×9＋3×3 sz
Price from **5300** rbls

SECTION on BA Axis

PLAN for No 38

PROJECT No 39

Stable and Storage

Area 3×3 sz

Price from **700** rbls

CROSS-SECTION

PLAN

Cows

Horses

Carriages
and
Storage

Hay

Saddles

Calves

Chickens

Laying
Hens

Geese

Larder

Cow | Storage

Horse

Horse

Project No 40

Stable and storage.

This includes a wood-storage area between the stable and carriage-house - separated from the carriage house by a wooden wall. For the building's construction details see the plans for Projects 38 and 39.

Project No 41

Greenhouse.

This building's structural details are clearly seen from the drawing. The building will require the following quantities of fire resistant bricks: basement - 12.6 cubic sazhens; foundation walls - 0.14 cubic sazhens (a total of 4,200 units). Irrigation pipes will also be needed.

Materials:
Wooden logs, 4.5 vershoks wide, 4 sazhens long – 20 units.
Wooden logs   3   "   3 sazhens long – 16 units
Roof timbers   3   "   4 sazhens long – 12 units
Panels 2 duim thick for floors and ceilings   - 20 items
Finishing materials for façade   - 25 units
Total glass   - 17 sq sazhens

The air gap between the inner greenhouse walls and the outer earth walls should be filled with soft terracotta (clay) to protect against ground water.

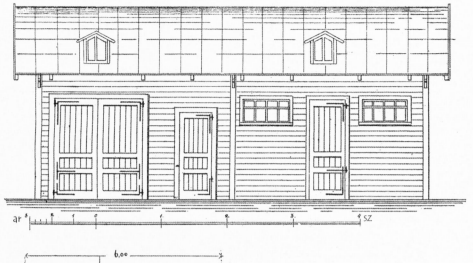

PROJECT No 40

Stable and Storage

Area 3×6 sz
Price from **1700** rbls

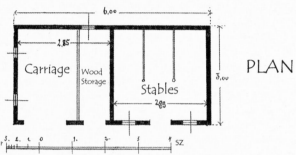

Carriage | Wood Storage | Stables

6,00
2,85
3,00
2,89

PLAN

CROSS-SECTION

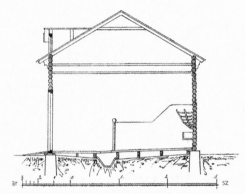

FACADE

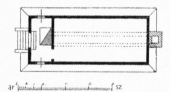

PLAN

PROJECT No 41

Greenhouse

Area 2×5 sz
Price from **900** rbls

SIDE ELEVATION

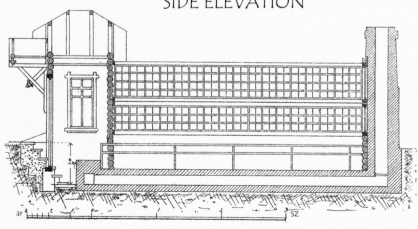

CROSS-SECTION

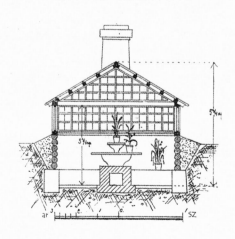

Project No 42

Basic swimming house.

This is built over existing water with a retractable privacy box, able to be lowered on chains. The building stands on columns; the walls are made from wooden panels with exterior decorative features.

Project No 43

Small swimming house.

It stands on four floating boxed columns, attached to the river bank by cables. Very comfortable and easy to remove from the river in winter. To make the structure lighter the wall panels can be made of fabric or platted material, etc.

Project No 44

Cowshed for 10 cows.

The function of the building should be clear from the plan. The façade shows two rooms on the second floor – one is a poultry house with areas for egg incubation, egg storage and feathers. The other is a milk room.

PROJECT No 42

Swimming House on Columns
Area 3 x 4 sz
Price from **400** rbls

FRONT FACADE

SIDE ELEVATION

PLAN

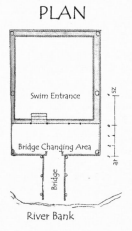

SIDE ELEVATION

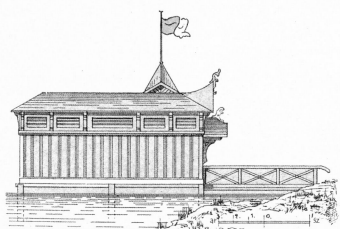

FACADE

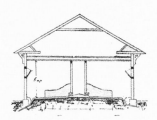

CROSS-SECTION

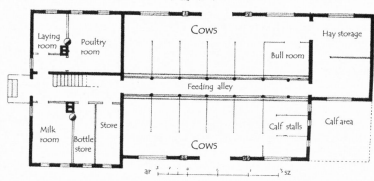

PROJECT No 43

Floating Swimming House
Area 2×3 sz
Price from **450** rbls

FRONT FACADE

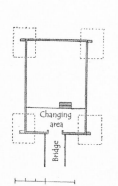

PROJECT No 44

Shed for 10 Cows
Area 3×5＋5×8 sz
Price from **6700** rbls

PLAN

Project No 45

Earthen food storage house with two concentric internal areas - the inner is designed for ice. In the summer when the ice melts, the stairs and partition are removable. The details of this can be seen on the section plan.

They call this building 'a stomach'. It is designed to be surrounded by earth on all sides, preferably peat. Materials: 3.5 vershoks of wooden logs; beams (135 units); 2.5 duim panels for the floor and 60 units for the roof. The size of hole required for the 'stomach' is 2.50 cubic sazhens. The amount of earth required is 20 cubic sazhens.

Project No 46

When the ground surface is peat this storage area is better made above ground. This project contains two rooms:

a) External room 3.5-4 vershoks logs layered with earth, including a warm double-ceiling sealed with mastic.

b) Internal room - made from layers of earth with air gaps. The internal rooms should be located as close to the north-west corner of the building as possible. This is because the air gap on the west and south-facing walls receives more sun, leaving the space directly below warmer. The space between the two interior rooms on the west and south sides should be 2 arshins. It is best to finish the surfaces with a mixture of terracotta clay and wooden chips. The thickness should be 4-5 vershoks

The innermost room has an extra panelled ceiling, sealed with mastic. This space is divided into three small areas each containing ice.

1) Freezer or cold room, for food storage.

2) Storage area for ice

3) Long term storage area for ice with a double door. The far side of this room contains a small window for refilling the ice.

Ice House Food-storage

Area 2×3 sz

Price from **500** rbls

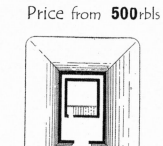

PROJECT No 46

Above Ground Storage

Area 3×3 sz

Price from **800** rbls

HORIZONTAL SECTION № 45.

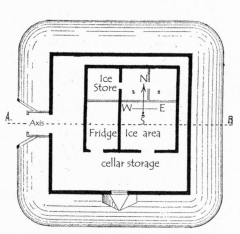

PLAN

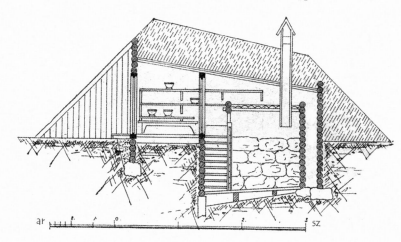

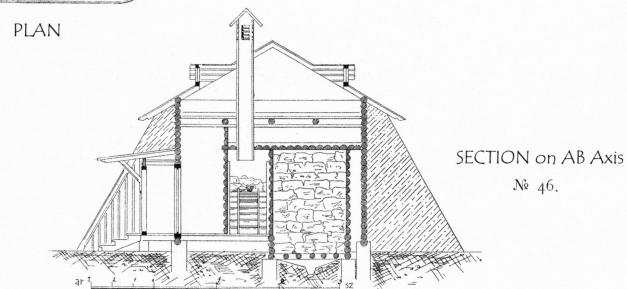

SECTION on AB Axis

№ 46.

GARDEN ARCHITECTURE

Pavilions
Storage Sheds
Pergolas
Gates
Low Gates
Fences

Project No 47

Garden pavilion. Well suited for a forested area. Could also be used as a small summer house or a sales pavilion - in which case the interior could carry tables. The design is meant to be versatile. The rear could be used as a storage room from where stairs could be built to the upper balcony.

Project No 48

Pergola. The floor is best constructed from two wooden panels and stood on an old tree stump. The pergola stairs are wooden logs and the roof should appear like a straw hat.

Project No 49

This design of a Norwegian-style garden shed also contains a possible living area. The structure is made from logs finished with planks and decorated with small, 2 duim thick wooden straps and columns.

To economise, the front of the non-living section could be built out of simple wooden panels and used as in Project 47.

Project No 50

Mauritanian-style octagonal pergola. The columns are finished with 1 duim thick wood panels. All connections and gaps should be thoroughly rendered. When painted in white and set on grass it gives the appearance of a marble pergola.

PROJECT No 47

Garden Pavilion

PLAN № 47.

storage area

sales counter

PLAN № 49.

Kitchen

Room

selling area

PROJECT No 48

Pergola on Tree Stump

PROJECT No 50

Garden Pergola

PROJECT No 49

Fruit Storage Shed

PLAN № 50.

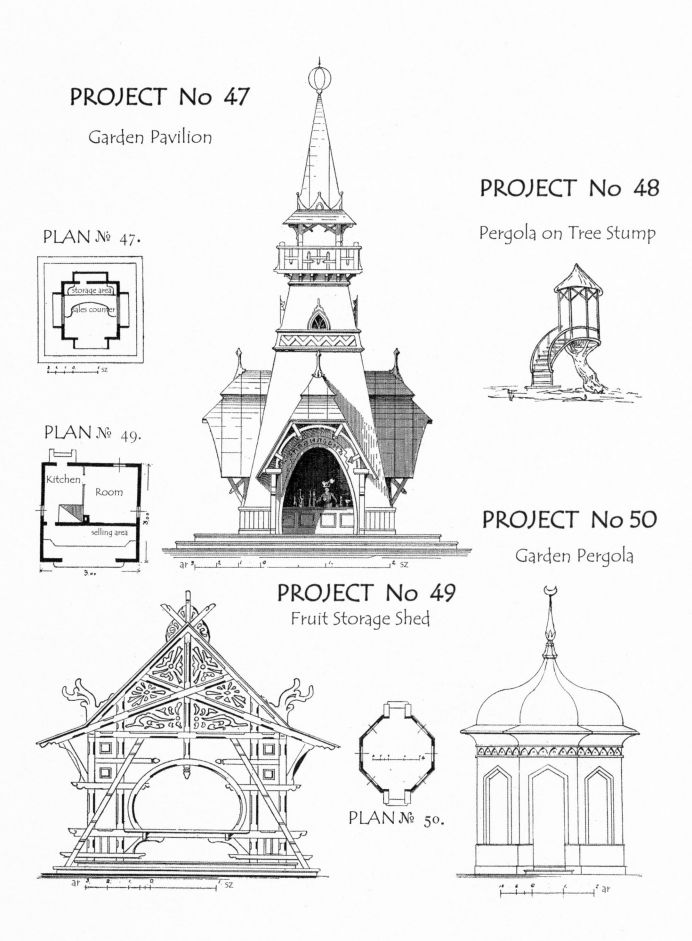

Project No 51

Pergola with round balcony. This design is based around four main log pillars, with flooring radiating outward from the centre.

Project No 52

Summer garden pergola. The walls are finished with a rustic-style wood; the window openings on all four sides have the option of carrying window sills. Tables can be placed under the fabric shutters.

Project No 53

Chinese-style pergola, finished in flat surfaced wood.

Project No 54

Mauritanian-style pergola. All columns are finished with wood siding. A decorative wire grill is used under the upper cornices.

Project No 55

Pergola. One siting of this rectangular pergola could be above an earth storage house. It is supported by 16 columns, boxed in by rendered wood panels. Wood planking is used for the base. The roof is arched and requires 2 duim thick timber roofing panels to give a lace-like effect. The upper roof is of wood panels, 0.33 – 0.25 duim thick, surfaced by tin sheets.

Project No 56

Pergola with canopy for protection against the sun and rain. Finished on all sides by wood panels with fabric shutters, the pergola is also removable.

The two central columns require logs 3 sazhens long which we advise cutting in half. The four outer columns are 3 sazhens long (not requiring cutting). These should be fixed from below and above then finished with wood panelling. The roof is made of wood panels (1 duim thick, 40 units) as metal sheeting would be too hot.

PROJECT No 51

Garden Pergola

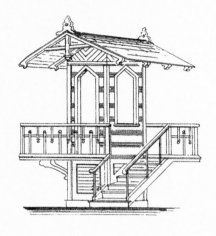

PROJECT No 52

Garden Pavilion

PROJECT No 53

Garden Pergola

PROJECT No 54

Garden Pergola

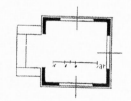

PROJECT No 55

Garden Pergola

PROJECT No 56

Shuttered Pergola

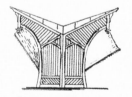

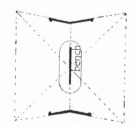

Project No 57

Entrance gate topped by pergola. The stairs are positioned on the gate's right-hand side. All columns and neckings are made from 4 vershok-wide wood. The spaces between columns are decoratively filled with wooden planking.

Project No 58

Solid gate.

Project No 59

The left-hand side of this gate contains solid panels. Its upper part uses three differently designed opening sections. The right-hand side is made from open-posted gate panels.

Project No 60

Another version of the open-posted gate.

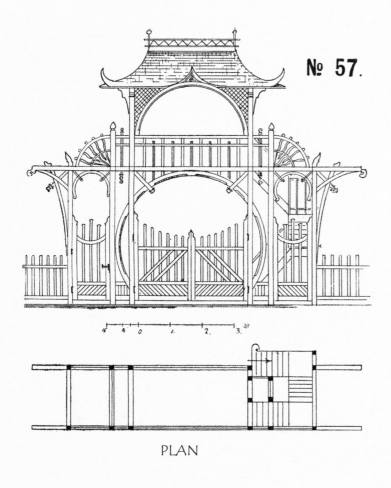

№ 57.

PLAN

№ 58.

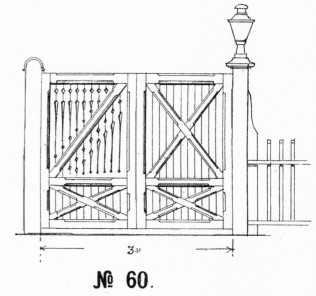

3 ar

№ 60.

№ 59.

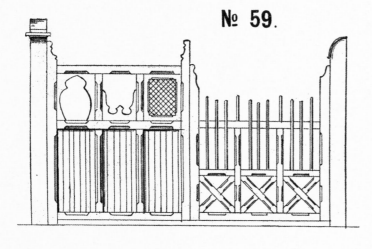

SCALE

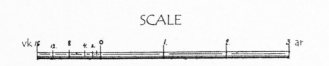

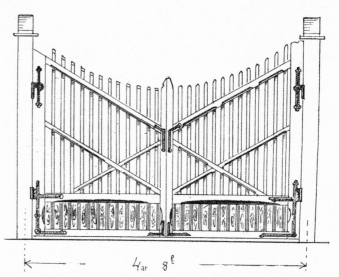

4 ar 8 ℓ

Project Nos 61 and 62

Fence types made from tree branches nailed together.

Example of a small summer house plot

Ideas for the positioning of house, garden and utility buildings.

Project No 64

Light fence with rendered wood posts.

Project No 66

An attractive, cheap fence. The base is made from 1 duim diameter wooden planks; the space between the posts is filled with wire box-frames.

Project No 67

Simple but solid fence made from tree logs.

№ 61.

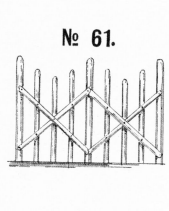

№ 62.

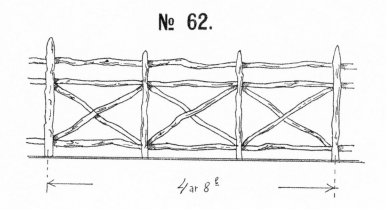

4 ar 8^{e}

Demonstration Layout
for Small Plot

Rear Neighbour

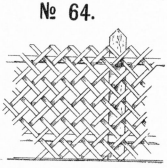

№ 63.

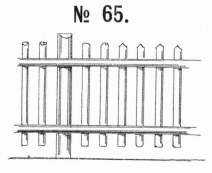

A – House
B – Underground Storage (Ice House)
C – Cow Storage
D – Wood Storage
E – Stable and Hay Storage
F – Poultry House
G – Servants' House
H – Well
I – Septic Tank

№ 64.

№ 65.

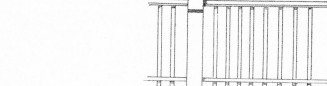

№ 66.

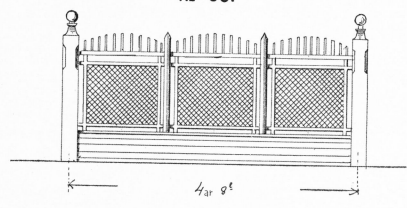

4 ar 8^{e}

№ 67.

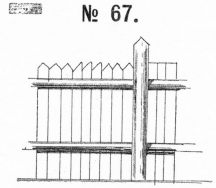

Project No 68

Small garden gate, Norwegian-style.

Project No 69

Simple fence made from natural, non-processed branches and barbed wire. The fence is given stability by the horizontal branches.

Project No 72

Solid fence made with decoratively cut and painted, 1.5 duim thick wooden planks.

Project No 74

Rectangular posted fence, 2 duim in width, secured top and bottom by horizontal planks.

Project No 75

Varying sized wooden planks employing decorative motifs, fixed on horizontal planks, some with spaces, some without, to form solid or spaced patterns.

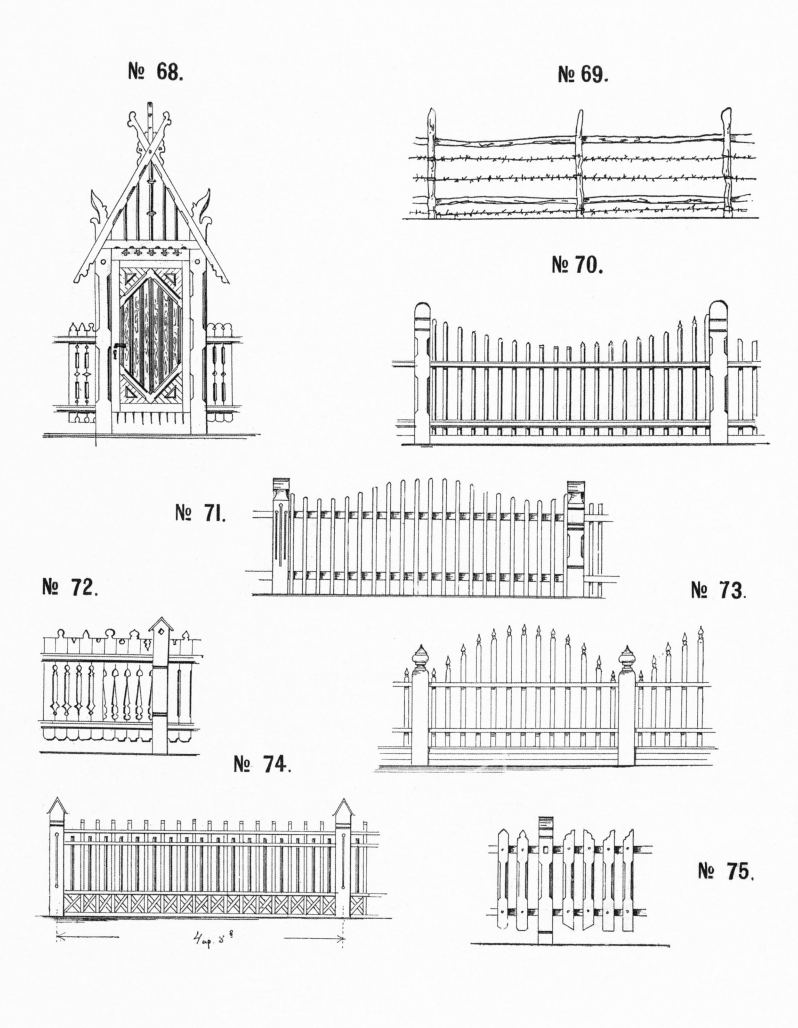

№ 68.

№ 69.

№ 70.

№ 71.

№ 72.

№ 73.

№ 74.

№ 75.

Books By The Same Author:

Cheap Buildings, edition 1, 46 projects of wooden and stone summer-houses, rental houses and garden utility buildings, with an annex of two school designs. 2nd edition – price 2 roubles.

Cheap Buildings, volume 2, 4th edition - 3 roubles.

Cheap Buildings, volume 3, 3rd edition – price 2 roubles.

Cheap Buildings, volume 4, projects for; summer houses, log houses, stone houses, mixed pergolas, fences, gates, all in different styles. Price 2 roubles 50 kopeks.

Interior Design. Designs for living rooms, tables, offices, toilets, bedrooms, bathrooms, lighting, walls, with explanatory text. Price 4 roubles.

Windows and Doors. 110 examples of window and door designs, balconies, fences, pergolas, flower baskets in various styles. Price 3 roubles.

City House Facades. 42 examples of facades and plans for rental houses, office buildings, private flats, and architectural details. Price 1 rouble. Publisher P Soykin.

Warm, wooden plank house. Project with explanatory text. Price 50 kopeks. Publisher P Soykin.

Garden Architecture Motifs. 167 sketches of garden pergolas, pavilions, fences, gates, small gates, bridges, garden furniture and decoration. Price 50 kopeks. Publisher P Soykin.

Publications in Progress

Cheap Buildings. 5th edition. Stone houses in different styles, price 3 roubles 50 kopeks.

Planned Publications

Public Buildings. Projects of public schools, hospitals, office buildings, and public street buildings.

Metal grill design. Sketches of metal-grill design for windows, doors, fences, etc.

A full list of the completed buildings made by the author of this book will be listed in a specially produced edition – soon to be published under the title **'THE PRACTICAL BUILDER.'**

AVIS

Should you wish to order any project with an estimate, please answer the listed questions below. This will save you the trouble of having to write further letters of inquiry. Please give precise answers to each question.

SEND BY POST

1. **General plan** (or copy) of the plot with borders of neighbour's property. Location of the lot (region, city, town etc). Address of the landlord.

PLEASE INDICATE

2. The approximate price of the building and of what kind (its purpose and type – ie, stone, wooden logs, wooden panels, etc).

3. Desired size of house and rooms (approximate). The quantity and purpose of rooms; number of floors; with or without basement (living or non-living).

4. Upper-floor made with either wooden logs or panels. Whether the floors are made into one or two separate flats.

5. Foundations, solid or set on posts - of granite, stone, concrete or brick (depending on available local materials).

6. Floor and mastic type (earth floor, log floor, wooden plank or panel, simple or parquet, etc).

7. Height of each storey. We recommend no less than 4.5 arshins.

8. Height of floor above the ground (we recommend no less than 1 arshin).

9. What kind of roofing (tin, tarred, tile, etc).

10. Type of oven (metal, tiles, etc).

11. Type of bathroom and warm-water closet.

12. Type of piped water system and from what source.

13. Type of house exterior (with finishing or without, rendered, painted, etc).

14. Ceilings (rendered or finished with wooden panels or planks).

15. Partitions (double or single; rendered or hardboard, etc).

16. Oven fixtures, window fixtures (iron, metal, etc).

17. Paintwork (what kind and how you wish it painted).

18. Glasswork (what kind of glass).

19. Doors and windows (quantity of double and single doors; style of design - decorated, rustic, etc, window frames, inward or outward opening).

20. Special requests (concrete basements, wells, artesian wells, ice storage, etc).

21. General planning (levelling the plot), clearing the plot, creating drainage, garden work, etc.

22. Utility Buildings. Purpose and type.

NOTE: HISTORICAL INFORMATION ONLY. THIS COMPANY NO LONGER EXISTS.

GLOSSARY OF MEASUREMENTS

1 duim [dm]   = 2.54cm
1 vershok [vk]   = 4.4 cm
1 arshin [ar]   = 70.4 cm
1 sazhen [sz]   = 2.1336 m

1 rouble [rbl] (early 1917) = $20 US (today) very roughly.

See the 'A Sustainable Architecture' section of the Introduction.

EDITOR'S NOTE

The style and formatting of this translated edition have been kept as close as possible to the Russian original, even at the expense of some more logical design choices. The page geometry is more 1917 than today, as are the fonts and their spacing. Most inconsistencies of design and editing have been left in rather than replaced - as with a few numbers that appear without their units. Some of the Russian letters used in the original are no longer found today: this includes the measurement system - see Glossary. A few pieces of Russian still remain on the pages, due either to size or space constraints. The vernacular of some translated sentences may appear archaic, but this is kept to remain truer to the period in which they were composed. Occasionally they have been slightly condensed, but only better to retain their original meaning.

The details and descriptions of the graphics have been translated from pre-Revolutionary terminology - a time when electricity was considered a luxury in the countryside. Some meanings have changed slightly. The 'ground floor' in the text refers to the '1st floor' in the drawings.

As the original edition was clearly rushed into print just before the Revolution, several projects were printed without explanations - such as Project 9. A few words have been added here, purely to balance the page. The other lesser projects remain uncollated. As a result the book retains some of its slightly chaotic production values due, as the editor's note explains at the start, to its re-formatting in the face of the 1917 paper shortages.

The spelling of the author's surname - Story - has been set according to the most common British rendition of the name, rather than the direct transliteration from the Russian - Stori. This is in the absence of any other solid evidence of how he might have wished it spelt in English.

At the risk of stating the obvious, readers should be aware that the company whose works are advertised here is long departed. Please do not order any cheap buildings from the address provided!